MANCAT LIBRARY

061574

NOTES

A MIDSU[barcode D0246433]R
NIGHT'S DREAM

WILLIAM SHAKESPEARE

MANCAT
Wythenshawe Sixth Form
Newall Green Centre
Greenbow Road
Wythenshawe
MANCHESTER
M23 2SX

NOTES BY JOHN SCICLUNA

MANCAT
COLLEGE LIBRARIES
ASHTON OLD ROAD
MANCHESTER
M11 2WH

 Longman

 York Press

The right of John Scicluna to be identified as Author of this Work
has been asserted by him in accordance with the
Copyright, Designs and Patents Act 1988

YORK PRESS
322 Old Brompton Road, London SW5 9JH

PEARSON EDUCATION LIMITED
Edinburgh Gate, Harlow,
Essex CM20 2JE, United Kingdom
Associated companies, branches and representatives throughout the world

© Librairie du Liban *Publishers* 1997, 2002

All rights reserved. No part of this publication may be reproduced, stored
in a retrieval system, or transmitted in any form or by any means, electronic,
mechanical, photocopying, recording, or otherwise, without either the prior
written permission of the Publishers or a licence permitting restricted copying
in the United Kingdom issued by the Copyright Licensing Agency Ltd,
90 Tottenham Court Road, London W1P 9HE

First published 1997
This new and fully revised edition first published 2002

10 9 8 7 6 5 4 3 2 1

ISBN 0–582–50615–8

Designed by Michelle Cannatella
Illustrated by Gilly Marklew
Typeset by Land & Unwin (Data Sciences), Bugbrooke, Northamptonshire
Produced by Addison Wesley Longman China Limited, Hong Kong

CONTENTS

York Notes are designed to give you a broader perspective on works of literature studied at GCSE and equivalent levels. With examination requirements changing in the twenty-first century, we have made a number of significant changes to this new series. We continue to help students to reach their own interpretations of the text but York Notes now have important extra-value new features.

You will discover that York Notes are genuinely interactive. The new **Checkpoint** features make sure that you can test your knowledge and broaden your understanding. You will also be directed to excellent websites, books and films where you can follow up ideas for yourself.

The **Resources** section has been updated and an entirely new section has been devoted to how to improve your grade. Careful reading and application of the principles laid out in the Resources section guarantee improved performance.

The **Detailed summaries** include an easy-to-follow skeleton structure of the story-line, while the section on **Language and style** has been extended to offer an in-depth discussion of the writer's techniques.

The Contents page shows the structure of this study guide. However, there is no need to read from the beginning to the end as you would with a novel, play or poem. Use the Notes in the way that suits you. Our aim is to help you with your understanding of the work, not to dictate how you should learn.

Our authors are practising English teachers and examiners who have used their experience to offer a whole range of **Examiner's secrets** – useful hints to encourage exam success.

The General Editor of this series is John Polley, Senior GCSE Examiner and former Head of English at Harrow Way Community School, Andover.

The author of these Notes is John Scicluna, who, having studied English and Drama, began teaching in 1967. Since that time he has been actively involved in the teaching of English and English Literature to secondary age pupils.

The text used in these Notes is the New Penguin Shakespeare Edition, 1967, edited by Stanley Wells.

PART ONE

INTRODUCTION

HOW TO STUDY A PLAY

Though it may seem obvious, remember that a play is written to be performed before an audience. Ideally, you should see the play live on stage. A film or video recording is next best, though neither can capture the enjoyment of being in a theatre and realising that your reactions are part of the performance.

There are six aspects of a play:

❶ THE PLOT: a play is a story whose events are carefully organised by the playwright in order to show how a situation can be worked out

❷ THE CHARACTERS: these are the people who have to face this situation. Since they are human they can be good or bad, clever or stupid, likeable or detestable, etc. They may change too!

❸ THE THEMES: these are the underlying messages of the play, e.g. jealousy can cause the worst of crimes; ambition can bring the mightiest low

❹ THE SETTING: this concerns the time and place that the author has chosen for the play

❺ THE LANGUAGE: the writer uses a certain style of expression to convey the characters and ideas

❻ STAGING AND PERFORMANCE: the type of stage, the lighting, the sound effects, the costumes, the acting styles and delivery must all be decided

Work out the choices the dramatist has made in the first four areas, and consider how a director might balance these choices to create a live performance.

The purpose of these York Notes is to help you understand what the play is about and to enable you to make your own interpretation. Do not expect the study of a play to be neat and easy: plays are chosen for examination purposes, not written for them!

DID YOU KNOW?

When studying a play, it is easy to forget that it was meant to be performed and seen, not just read. If you can, go and see *A Midsummer Night's Dream* at the theatre – as Shakespeare intended!

AUTHOR – LIFE AND WORKS

1564 William Shakespeare is baptised on 26 April in Stratford-on-Avon, Warwickshire

1582 Marries Anne Hathaway

1583 Birth of daughter, Susanna

1585 Birth of twins, Hamnet and Judith

1590–3 Early published works and poems written when theatres are closed by Plague

1593–4 *A Midsummer Night's Dream* thought to have been written

1594 Joins Lord Chamberlain's Men (from 1603 named the King's Men) as actor and playwright

1595–99 Writes the history plays and comedies

1597 Shakespeare buys New Place, the second biggest house in Stratford

1599 Moves to newly-opened Globe Theatre

1599–1608 Writes his greatest plays, including *Macbeth*, *King Lear* and *Hamlet*

1600 *A Midsummer Night's Dream* first printed

1608–13 Takes over the lease of Blackfriars Theatre and writes final plays, the romances, ending with *The Tempest*

1609 Shakespeare's sonnets published

1613 Globe Theatre burns down 29 June, during performance of *Henry VIII*

1616 Shakespeare dies, 23 April, and is buried in Stratford

1623 First Folio of Shakespeare's plays published

CONTEXT

1558 Elizabeth I becomes Queen of England

1568 Mary Queen of Scots is imprisoned for life

1577–80 Sir Francis Drake becomes the first to circumnavigate the world

1587 Mary Queen of Scots is executed

1588 Defeat of the Spanish Armada

1591 Tea is first drunk in England

1593–94 Outbreak of the Plague in London, closing theatres and killing as many as 5,000 people, according to some sources

1594 Queen Elizabeth spends Christmas at Greenwich and is entertained by the leading theatre company of her day, headed by James Burbage, William Kempe and Shakespeare

1595 Walter Raleigh sails to Guiana

1599 Oliver Cromwell is born

1603 Elizabeth I dies on 24 March; James I, son of Mary, succeeds to throne of England

1604 Peace treaty signed with Spain

1605 The Gunpowder Plot

1611 The Bible is translated into the Authorised (King James) Version

1614 Fire sweeps through Stratford but New Place is spared

1618 Thirty Years War begins

SETTING AND BACKGROUND

SHAKESPEARE'S BACKGROUND

Family life

On 26 April 1564 William Shakespeare, the eldest son of John Shakespeare and his wife Mary, was christened at Holy Trinity Church in Stratford upon Avon. There is no exact record of his date of birth but, by tradition, we normally celebrate his birthday on 23 April, which is the Feast of St George.

John and Mary Shakespeare had a total of three sons and four daughters, but only William's sister Joan is mentioned in his will, so it is possible that all the others died at quite a young age. William almost certainly attended the local grammar school, where he would have studied Latin and the Latin authors.

In November 1582 William married Anne Hathaway. Their first child, Susanna, was born in May 1583 and in 1585 they had twins, Hamnet and Judith. Hamnet died when he was only eleven but the two daughters lived to marry and to have children of their own.

Life in the theatre

Little is known about what Shakespeare did to earn a living in Stratford, but by the late 1580s he was an established actor and playwright in London. Shakespeare worked mainly with a group of actors known as the Lord Chamberlain's Men. The company included Richard Burbage, who had the reputation of being the greatest actor of his time, and they performed at The Theatre, the first purpose built playhouse in England. In 1608 the company became the King's Men. They took over the Blackfriars Theatre which had better facilities than the Globe, and they were also much in favour at court.

Later life

Shakespeare did not lose touch with Stratford altogether. In 1596 he gained the right to a coat of arms and in 1597 he bought a very large house in Stratford called New Place; and seems to have retired to spend most of his time in Stratford from about 1610. He continued to make visits to London and it was on one of these occasions, at the first

DID YOU KNOW?
John Shakespeare was a glove-maker who was an alderman and later a bailiff of Stratford. John's wife, Mary, was the daughter of a local landowner called Arden.

DID YOU KNOW?
Shakespeare's wife, Anne Hathaway, was some eight years older than he was.

DID YOU KNOW?
Shakespeare died on his (traditional) birthday.

DID YOU KNOW?

It is generally believed that Shakespeare was commissioned to write *A Midsummer Night's Dream* to be performed at a wedding – rather like the workmen!

performance of his play *Henry VIII* in 1613, that the Globe theatre caught fire and burned to the ground.

Shakespeare died in Stratford upon Avon on St George's Day, 23 April 1616. He was buried in the local church, where a monument on the north wall was erected to commemorate the town's most famous son.

THE SUPERNATURAL

Shakespeare used a variety of settings for his plays, so it is not unusual to find that *A Midsummer Night's Dream* is set in ancient Athens. Shakespeare would never have been to Greece but he would have been familiar with many of the mythological and historical characters of that country. Many of his plays are based upon well-known stories that he adapted to his own use, though it is quite possible that *A Midsummer Night's Dream* is Shakespeare's own. In Elizabethan England most people still lived, worked or had strong links with the countryside. Folk stories and legends of fairies, ghostly spirits and strange supernatural creatures were common, and so the fairy world of Oberon and Titania would not have seemed particularly strange to the audiences of that time. The title of the play and the mention in Act IV, Scene 1 of 'The rite of May', are references to festivals of Tudor times.

LOVE

The theme of love provides opportunities for comedy and serious social comment. By using the wedding of Theseus and Hippolyta, two noble characters from classical Greek legend, as his starting point Shakespeare was able to give the play a feeling of importance. Shakespeare's audience would also have seen in their story an affirmation of the dominant role of the husband over the wife, an idea which they saw as a part of the natural law. Theseus himself makes his physical superiority over Hippolyta clear when he says:

CHECKPOINT 1

Why did the Elizabethan audience need to use its imagination?

'Hippolyta, I wooed thee with my sword / And won thy love doing thee injuries.'   (I.1.16–17)

A similar theme may be found in other Shakespeare plays.

THE THEATRE

An Elizabethan audience would have usually gone to the theatre in the afternoon. Specially built playhouses such as the Globe were a relatively new idea. These buildings had tiered galleries where the spectators could sit. This covered seating was built around an open area into which the stage, which had a balcony and a higher gallery, jutted out. Some of the audience would stand in the open area in front and round the stage. Since the theatre was quite small and the stage quite big, it meant that everyone could see and hear very clearly.

THE WOODS

The night-time woods provide a strange and confusing environment for the four lovers and for the workmen, while being somewhere that the mystical fairies can seem perfectly at home – a place of hidden events, strange happenings and mysterious creatures. With the woods, Shakepeare creates an ideal setting for the strangeness and unreality of *A Midsummer Night's Dream*.

DID YOU KNOW?
The Globe Theatre in London is a reconstruction of the original Elizabethan structure – well worth a visit!

Now take a break!

What happens	Who is involved		
	Court & lovers	Fairies	Workmen
1 Theseus plans to marry Hippolyta.	♥		
2 Egeus complains about his daughter's disobedience.	♥		
3 Hermia and Lysander decide to elope.	♥		
4 Quince gathers his workmen to cast their play.			🖐
5 Oberon and Titania argue.		✿	
6 Oberon decides to use magic.		✿	
7 Demetrius chases Hermia and Lysander into the woods.	♥		
8 Demetrius is followed by Helena.	♥		
9 Oberon decides to help Helena.	♥	✿	
10 Oberon obtains and uses love-juice on Titania.		✿	
11 Hermia and Lysander fall asleep and Puck mistakenly puts the love-juice on Lysander's eyes.	♥	✿	
12 Helena wakes Lysander, who falls in love with her.	♥		
13 Hermia wakes to find Lysander has gone, she looks for him.	♥		
14 The workmen rehearse the play in the woods.			🖐
15 Puck gives Bottom an ass's head.		✿	🖐
16 The other workmen run away from Bottom.			🖐
17 Bottom's singing wakes Titania and she falls in love with him.		✿	🖐

What happens	Who is involved		
	Court & lovers	Fairies	Workmen
18 Bottom enjoys the attention of Titania and her fairies.		❀	☞
19 Oberon realises that Puck has made a mistake and given the love-juice to the wrong Athenian.	♥	❀	
20 Oberon scolds Puck and enchants Demetrius.	♥	❀	
21 Demetrius also falls in love with Helena.	♥		
22 Hermia and Helena argue.	♥		
23 Puck separates the four lovers and releases Lysander from the spell.	♥	❀	
24 Oberon gets the changeling child from Titania.		❀	
25 Titania is released from the love-spell and she is horrified at Bottom's appearance.		❀	☞
26 Oberon and Titania are reconciled.		❀	
27 The Athenian lovers wake, and each couple is happily reunited and married.	♥		
28 Bottom sleeps and wakes to find Titania gone.		❀	☞
29 The workmen bemoan Bottom's absence.			☞
30 Bottom returns looking normal.			☞
31 The workmen's play is chosen and they perform it at the triple wedding celebrations.	♥		☞
32 Oberon, Titania and the fairies celebrate and bless the human marriages.	♥	❀	

PART TWO

SUMMARIES

GENERAL SUMMARY

ACT I

Theseus, the Duke of Athens, is preparing for his wedding to Hippolyta, Queen of the Amazons.

EXAMINER'S SECRET

You will not get high marks by simply re-telling the story.

Egeus wants his daughter, Hermia, to marry Demetrius. Hermia, however, is in love with Lysander and they decide to elope. Hermia's friend Helena is herself in love with Demetrius. She decides to gain favour with him by telling him of the elopement.

A group of Athenian workmen meet to cast a play that they hope to perform as part of Theseus's wedding celebrations. They decide to rehearse their play in the woods, away from any possible observers.

ACT II

In the woods, Oberon and Titania, the king and queen of the fairies, are involved in a bitter quarrel. Oberon puts love-juice from a magic flower on Titania's eyes, so that she will fall in love with the first creature that she sees when she wakes up.

Demetrius goes into the woods in search of Hermia. When Helena declares her love to him, Demetrius treats her cruelly and rejects her. Oberon tells Puck to use some of the love-juice on Demetrius so that when he wakes up he will fall in love with Helena. Puck puts the spell on the sleeping Lysander, mistaking him for Demetrius. Helena wakes Lysander and he falls in love with her. Lysander chases after Helena and Hermia sets off to find Lysander.

DID YOU KNOW?

Only three of Shakespeare's plays are shorter than *A Midsummer Night's Dream*.

ACT III

The workmen rehearse their play in the woods. Puck sees a chance for some good practical jokes. He bewitches the chief actor, Bottom, giving him an ass's head, and the other workmen run away. Bottom's singing wakes Titania and she immediately falls in love with him.

Oberon is delighted when Puck tells him of Titania's love for Bottom, but soon realises that Puck has put the spell on the wrong man. When Demetrius falls asleep, Oberon puts the love spell on him and sends Puck to bring Helena. When Demetrius wakes up, he too falls in love with Helena. She is convinced that both the young men are cruelly pretending to be in love with her, and that Hermia is in on the joke too. Hermia, on the other hand, is convinced that Helena has stolen Lysander from her and they argue. Demetrius and Lysander go off to fight over Helena. Puck separates the four lovers and releases Lysander from the spell so he is no longer in love with Helena.

The quarrel between Oberon and Titania is resolved so Oberon releases Titania from the spell. Puck returns Bottom's appearance to normal.

ACT IV

When the four lovers are woken it is clear that Demetrius is in love with Helena, and that Hermia still wishes to marry Lysander. Theseus announces that the two couples will be married at the same time as Hippolyta and himself. None of the four young people is quite sure if the events of the night really happened or were merely dreams.

Bottom wakes up and rejoins the workmen. He promises to tell them about his adventures after they have prepared for the play.

ACT V

Theseus chooses the workmen's play as the entertainment for the evening. The workmen make many mistakes and perform rather badly but the courtiers are entertained. After everyone has retired to bed, Oberon and Titania bless the newly-married couples and the fairies dance through the palace in a celebration of harmony.

CHECK THE BOOK

Look at Chaucer's *The Knight's Tale* and *Legend of Good Women* to see how they might have influenced the plot of *A Midsummer Night's Dream*.

DETAILED SUMMARIES

SCENE 1 – The argument over Hermia

1 Theseus and Hippolyta discuss their forthcoming marriage.

2 Egeus, Demetrius and Lysander argue over whom Hermia should marry.

3 Hermia and Lysander decide to elope.

4 Helena is in love with Demetrius and decides that she will tell him about 'fair Hermia's flight' (line 246).

As the slow passage of time is emphasised by words such as 'long','slow' and 'lingers' (lines 1–6), Theseus shows impatience for the arrival of their wedding day, which will be at the time of the next full moon (four days' time). There are several references to the moon throughout the play, which acts as a measurement of time. Night-time is important as the time of mystery and dreams, and the moon imagery that Shakespeare creates strengthens the dream-like quality of the events, as well as reflecting the powerful influence of an outside force on the activities of man.

> **CHECKPOINT 2**
>
> Think about the harshness of the Athenian law. What would happen to Hermia if she refused to marry Demetrius?

> **CHECKPOINT 3**
>
> How many different conflicts are apparent at the start of the play?

Theseus, the ruler of Athens, and Hippolyta, Queen of the Amazons, speak in a lyrical way about love and marriage, and introduce this as a major theme of the play. Yet Theseus and Hippolyta had faced each other on the battlefield when Theseus had defeated the invading Amazons, and this makes the suggestion, later voiced by Lysander, that 'The course of true love never did run smooth' (line 134). As we meet each set of characters we usually see that they are involved in conflicts of one sort or another, but throughout the play we also see that conflicts can be resolved and that harmony can prevail.

The men argue over Hermia

The wedding preparations are interrupted when Egeus arrives with his daughter Hermia, along with her two suitors: Lysander (whom Hermia loves) and Demetrius (her father's choice for her). Egeus's entrance strikes a note of discord. His manner is sharp and he refers to Hermia as if she is simply one of his possessions: 'she is mine' (line 97).

Lysander claims that he has more right to marry Hermia, saying that she returns his love and that his love is true whereas Demetrius is an 'inconstant man' (line 110) since he had previously declared that he loved Helena.

Both Theseus and Egeus represent very strong figures of authority, and as a result they feel able to direct events and to make judgements without discussion. Yet Theseus is also in love. He recognises Lysander's behaviour as being only what you might expect of a young man who is in love, and he does seem to have some sympathy with Hermia. He warns her of the dangers of disobeying her father, but he also offers her a less harsh alternative to the death penalty, gives her four days to think about her decision, and takes Egeus and Demetrius away, presumably to discuss the situation. His rather more even-handed approach helps us to realise that the important thing is that conflict exists, rather than which side we might take in an argument.

Hermia and Lysander reflect on the misery and suffering that 'crossed' lovers have to face, but Lysander's practical plan to run away to his

DID YOU KNOW?

Egeus's attitude to Hermia seems unacceptable to us, but it might have seemed more accceptable to an Elizabethan audience, who would have viewed Hermia's youthful passion as less reliable than the objective view of an older and, therefore, wiser man!

GLOSSARY

inconstant fickle

**CHECK
THE FILM**

Dead Poets Society
(1989) cites *A
Midsummer Night's
Dream* as an
example of young
people refusing to
conform.

**DID YOU
KNOW?**

Shakespeare was
very fond of the
soliloquy, which
appears regularly in
his tragedies.

aunt's home appears to offer a quick and easy solution. A plot, which
seemed to be moving in the direction of tragedy, is turned back so that
lightness and comedy can return. The lightness is emphasised by
Shakespeare's use of **rhyming couplets** from line 171 to the end of the
scene.

Helena's entrance shows another kind of suffering – that of someone
whose love is not returned. Helena's confusion and lack of self-
confidence about her appearance is made clear in her first words. She
makes a **pun** on the word 'fair' since Demetrius thinks that Hermia's
dark complexion and hair are more fair (beautiful) than Helena's
natural fair (light) colouring.

The way the two girls respond to each other's words (lines 194–201) –
echoing them, reversing them – shows us their friendship, while at the
same time highlighting the differences in their situations. The
closeness of the girls' relationship is made clearer when Helena is told
about the plan to elope. By taking Helena into their confidence,
Hermia and Lysander create the possibility for all the chaos that the
four lovers will face later. Furthermore, Hermia's betrayal by Helena
is a foretaste of her betrayal by Lysander.

Helena's **soliloquy** at the end of the scene makes it clear that love is
unreliable. It shows us the blind and irrational nature of love. 'Love
looks not with the eyes, but with the mind' (line 234) explains why
someone can see beauty where others would see none. This prepares
us for the effects of the love-juice on Lysander, Demetrius and, of
course, Titania. Helena's decision to tell Demetrius what Hermia and
Lysander are planning shows us that she too is blind to the truth:
bringing Demetrius and Hermia together again is not likely to
improve her own chances of regaining Demetrius's love.

SCENE 2 – The casting of the play

1 The workmen meet at Quince's house to cast the play.

2 Quince seems to be in charge but Bottom interrupts.

3 The actors agree to meet secretly in the woods.

A group of Athenian workmen – Quince the carpenter, Snug the joiner, Bottom the weaver, Flute the bellows-mender, Snout the Tinker and Starveling the tailor – meet to cast and rehearse the play of 'Pyramus and Thisbe'. They hope to perform the play as part of the Duke's wedding day celebrations. Quince seems to be in charge, and he calls out the part that he wants each man to act. The scene is a comic one. The humour comes mainly from the workmen's lack of understanding about how drama works. Bottom is keen and wants to play Pyramus, Thisbe and the lion, something which is clearly not possible. Quince is worried that Bottom would roar too ferociously and frighten the ladies, while Bottom claims that he could avoid that by roaring 'gently' (line 77). Quince's tact is seen when he persuades Bottom that Pyramus is such a fine, handsome man that only Bottom can play him. When Flute asks that he should not play a woman because 'I have a beard coming' (lines 43–4), we are reminded that in Shakespeare's time all the actors were male and so the younger actors played the women's parts.

DID YOU KNOW?

The workmen's scene is written in **prose**. Shakespeare frequently uses prose when writing scenes with ordinary, more humble, characters, even when the rest of the play is written in verse.

CHECKPOINT 4

Identify the occasions when Bottom interrupts the proceedings

Another source of humour lies in the workmen's misuse of words that they do not properly understand. Bottom says 'call them generally' (line 2) when he means 'call them individually'; he says 'I will aggravate my voice' (line 76) when he means 'moderate' it; he asks that they should rehearse 'obscenely' (line 100) when he means 'seemly'.

The title of their play, '*The most lamentable comedy and cruel death of Pyramus and Thisbe*', is strangely contradictory. In part the title suggests that the tragic tale of Pyramus and Thisbe will be turned into something funny by the workmen's naive acting of it, but it also suggests that **comedy** – as we have already seen in the previous scene and as we will see in the distortion of love that follows – can have tragic or painful elements (see **Themes**).

GLOSSARY

lamentable sad, distressing

Now take a break!

WHO SAYS ...?

1 'Full of vexation come I'

....

5 'Nay, faith, let me not play a woman – I have a beard coming.'

....

2 'If then true lovers have been ever crossed / It stands as an edict in destiny.'

....

4 'Things base and vile, holding no quantity, / Love can transpose to form and dignity.'

....

3 'Call you me fair? That "fair" again unsay.'

....

ABOUT WHOM?

6 'Stir up the Athenian youth to merriments.'

....

10 'You may do it extempore; for it is nothing but roaring.'

....

7 'Be advised, fair maid: / To you your father should be as a god.'

....

8 'But I beseech your grace that I may know / The worst that may befall me in this case'

....

9 'That's all one: you shall play it in a mask, and you may speak as small as you will.'

....

Check your answers on p. 77.

SCENE 1 – The fairies quarrel

1 Titania and Oberon argue over who should have the human Indian boy.

2 Oberon decides to enchant Titania with love-juice while she sleeps, so she will fall in love with the first thing she sees when she wakes.

3 Puck is sent to similarly bewitch Demetrius, so he will return Helena's love.

References to night and moonlight by Puck, Oberon and Demetrius establish the night-time setting of the scene. The play would originally have been performed in the daytime in a theatre without the benefit of lighting effects (see **Setting and background**). The setting is important since night-time is frequently associated with ideas of mystery, magic and insecurity. The mysterious effect of night-time, the woods and forces outside our control is the essential ingredient of the *Dream*.

CHECKPOINT 5

Find other references to night in the play.

The fairies in the wood

This scene introduces us to the fairies and the strange, mystical world in which they live. We learn that:

● Puck can change his shape and appearance, likes playing tricks and can move at great speed. Titania's servant fairy recognises Puck as a 'knavish sprite' (line 33).

● Oberon can make himself invisible, and has such keen eyesight that he has seen Cupid flying 'between the cold moon and the earth' (line 156). He understands – and knows how to use – the magical property of herbs and flowers.

● Oberon and Titania have a powerful influence on the course of nature. Their quarrels have led to the seasons losing their characteristic weather, causing confusion and hardship in the world.

The effects of the fairy quarreling on nature show that the world of the fairies may be different from that of man, but it is not completely separated from it. This idea is strengthened by the very human nature of the quarrels and the jealousy that exists over the alleged love affairs with humans. Despite Titania's concern about 'The human mortals' (line 101), she remains unwilling to hand over the child to Oberon.

Oberon wants to humiliate Titania. He wants her to fall in love with something ugly or repulsive. Helena has already alerted us to the way that love can make something 'base and vile' seem beautiful and attractive (I.1.232–3). The love-juice will have that exactly that effect on Titania's view of Bottom.

As we watch the four human lovers, we become more aware of how blind and irrational love is. Demetrius shows signs of insanity. His claim that he is 'wood within this wood' (line 192) is a **pun** on 'wood' meaning 'mad' and 'wood' meaning 'trees'. It echoes the feeling that love makes people behave irrationally.

When Puck returns with the magic flower, Oberon describes the place where he knows he will find Titania asleep. His lyrical description of the bower where Titania sleeps paints a picture of a beautiful place where nature is 'luscious' and 'sweet' (lines 251–2). The many references to nature would have had a great appeal to the audience in a mainly rural Elizabethan society. Oberon gives Puck part of the flower, and tells him that he will recognise the man (Demetrius) 'By the Athenian garments he hath on' (line 264). The audience knows that there is another young Athenian in the woods (Lysander), but Puck and Oberon are unaware of this. Here we have the beginning of the confusion.

> **DID YOU KNOW?**
> Mention of Cupid's unsuccessful attempt to shoot a love-arrow into the heart of an 'imperial votaress' (line 163) is possibly a reference to Queen Elizabeth I who, having refused all offers of marriage, was known as the Virgin Queen.

SCENE 2 – Titania and Lysander are bewitched

1 Titania falls asleep and Oberon puts the love-juice in her eyes.

2 Puck mistakes Lysander for Demetrius and puts the love-juice in his eyes.

3 Helena wakes up Lysander and he falls in love with her.

Titania gives her fairies various tasks to perform and asks them to sing her to sleep. Titania's instructions to the fairies to kill the pests that

DID YOU KNOW?

The fairies are sent off to keep owls away, and to gather bats' wings to make coats for elves. In Elizabethan times bats and owls were regarded as creatures of ill omen.

spoil roses reveal her concern for beauty in nature. The fairies are told to complete all the tasks in 'the third part of a minute' (line 2) and, like Puck's 'girdle round the earth / In forty minutes' (II.1.175–6), this suggests the speed at which fairies can travel.

The lullaby sung by the fairies gives the audience a short musical interlude, which adds to the magical quality of the setting. Although the song is about how the fairies will keep all evil, poisonous or harmful things away from Titania, the audience is aware of the irony in that Oberon is about to do harm to her. Oberon's spell, and his grim hopes about what might happen when Titania awakes, make a stark contrast to the opening of the scene.

Puck's mistake

Lysander and Hermia are lost and tired, and they decide to sleep for a while. Although Lysander claims that 'lying so, Hermia, I do not lie' (line 58), when he is woken up he instantly declares his love for Helena. In doing that he is clearly being unfaithful to Hermia and his love for Helena is itself a kind of lie. Ironically, the fact that Lysander and Hermia are keeping their distance while they sleep convinces Puck that he has found the right couple.

Puck's mistake starts off a confusing chain of events. Lysander claims that 'reason' has made him realise his love for Helena. Between lines 121 and 126 he mentions the word four times, yet the audience knows that reason has nothing to do with his change of heart. Helena cannot believe his expressions of love and thinks that he is showing 'mockery' and 'scorn' (lines 129–30). Lysander looks on the sleeping Hermia with contempt – further evidence of how unreasoning love can be.

Hermia wakes after a nightmare, in which a 'crawling serpent' (line 152) has been eating her heart while Lysander looked on smiling. Her dream is a powerful symbol of grief and despair at the outside force that has taken her love from her. Shakespeare shows us that while we may smile at the irrational behaviour of those who are under the influence of love, we must also recognise the pain felt by those who are hurt by it.

CHECKPOINT 6

Look at the different references to the heart in this scene.

Now take a break!

TEST YOURSELF (ACT II)

WHO SAYS ...?

1 'The fairy land buys not the child of me.'

....

5 'Methought a serpent ate my heart away'

....

2 'Thou shalt not from this grove / Till I torment thee for in injury.'

....

4 'O, that a lady of one man refused / Should of another therefore be abused!'

....

3 'I'll put a girdle round about the earth / In forty minutes!'

....

ABOUT WHOM?

6 'Do you amend it, then! It lies in you.'

....

10 'And run through fire I will for thy sweet sake!'

....

7 'Fetch me that flower – the herb I showed thee once.'

....

8 'And even for that do I love you the more.'

....

9 'For I am sick when I do look on thee.'

....

Check your answers on p. 77.

SCENE 1 – The rehearsal

1 In the woods, the men discuss how best to perform the play and please their audience.

2 Puck puts a spell on Bottom, giving him an ass's head.

3 The workmen are frightened and run away.

4 Bottom's singing wakes Titania and she falls in love with him.

The simplicity, awkwardness and very ordinary existence of the workmen are again shown by Shakespeare's use of **prose**. The prose contrasts starkly with the poetry and music of the fairies in the opening of the previous scene.

The workmen's mispronunciation and misuse of words, their failure to give each other the proper cues, and their fears that the audience will believe that the characters and events in their play are real, reveal their simplicity. They also hint at the exaggerated confidence that ignorance can give to any of us. The workmen's play is written in verse. It is rhythmic verse, which uses simple rhymes, but its use reflects the social standing of the characters of Pyramus and Thisbe. The poor quality of the verse suggests the poor job that these men are likely to make of producing a genuinely moving tragedy.

CHECKPOINT 7

Find examples of when the workmen misuse words.

CHECKPOINT 8

What is the reason for the workmen's play?

The workmen's simplicity makes them easy targets for Puck's kind of practical joke, and the ass's head that he puts on Bottom reflects Puck's opinion of the workmen's stupidity.

DID YOU KNOW?

Bottom's change in social status reflects the custom of popular festivals in Tudor times, where the rules of ordinary behaviour were set aside.

The rest of the workmen are frightened by Bottom's 'monstrous' appearance (line 108) and they run off. Snout and Quince each reappear briefly to tell Bottom he is 'changed' or 'translated' but Bottom has no idea of what has happened to his appearance – he thinks his friends are playing some sort of practical joke on him.

As Titania declares her love for Bottom, using words such as 'angel' (line 122), 'wise' and 'beautiful' (line 140), we realise how even someone as dignified and powerful as she is can be made a fool of love. This impression is strengthened when Bottom so readily accepts that anyone as beautiful as Titania can be so besotted by someone as rough and ready as him. He accurately observes that 'reason and love keep little company together nowadays' (lines 136–7). In that comment Bottom gives a clear reflection on what is happening in *A Midsummer Night's Dream*.

SCENE 2 – Chaos and confusion

❶ Puck tells Oberon that Titiania loves a man with an ass's head.

❷ It becomes clear that Puck has bewitched Lysander, not Demetrius.

❸ Oberon bewitches Demetrius so he too falls in love with Helena.

❹ The four lovers argue.

❺ The spell is taken off Lysander so he will no longer love Helena.

Puck explains to Oberon how he has placed an ass's head on the 'shallowest thickskin of that barren sort' (line 13), again emphasising Bottom's low social standing. Puck's account of Bottom's transformation, the workmen's reaction and Titania's falling in love with a 'monster' (line 6) clearly please Oberon. The vivid **imagery** that Puck uses, particularly that of wild geese and jackdaws scattering at the sound of a hunter's gun, makes the workmen's confusion and fear very real. The image of blind panic helps us to understand the workmen's belief that thorn bushes were living creatures grabbing at their clothes. The account of the confusion that Puck has caused among the workmen reminds us of what has happened and, with the appearance of Demetrius and Hermia, links that confusion with the chaos caused by Puck's mistake.

Oberon recognises the young man and realises the mistake that Puck has made. Oberon is determined to put matters right but Puck, on the other hand, seems pleased with the chaos his mistake is causing, When Oberon has placed the love-juice on the eyes of the sleeping Demetrius and Puck announces Helena's arrival we are ready for further confusion. Demetrius wakes and upon seeing Helena, he instantly proclaims his love for her. His first words to Helena, calling her 'goddess, nymph, perfect, divine' (line 137), are amusing as they contradict Lysander's claim that Demetrius does not love Helena. They also highlight again the irrational way that lovers behave. Demetrius continues with exaggerated descriptions of Helena's beauty. It is hardly surprising that Helena cannot understand the changes in the two men. Her belief that they are joined in a plot to make fun of her and that they both still love Hermia is perfectly logical.

> **? DID YOU KNOW?**
> A gun in the context of ancient Athens is an **anachronism** – it does not belong to the period in which it is depicted.

> **CHECKPOINT 9**
> Whose love remains constant, and who transfers his/her affections?

> **GLOSSARY**
> **shallowest thickskin** having least brain but thick-skinned like an animal

The two women quarrel. Helena's earlier recollections of their childhood (lines 198–219) have made it clear that she and Hermia were the closest of friends. Now she begs Hermia to remember their long friendship and to stop the pretence. It seems to her that Hermia has abandoned their 'ancient love' (line 215) and is involved in the plot. Hermia becomes more 'amazèd' (line 220) and says that it is Helena who is scorning her, not the other way round. Both Helena and Hermia feel betrayed and confused, and the two men are consumed by jealousy. Although the argument between the four young lovers becomes increasingly heated and angry, we can still see it as comic because we are aware of how the misunderstandings began and we are also aware that Oberon is available with the power to put things right.

Oberon begins to put things right

Oberon says that later their confusion 'Shall seem a dream and fruitless vision' (line 371). The four lovers will lose sight of what is real and what is not – rather like the workmen whom Puck had led on 'in this distracted fear' (line 31).

The future return of harmony is made clear when Oberon expresses his belief that Titania will now hand over the Indian boy, be released from her love for Bottom 'and all things shall be peace' (line 377).

The approach of Aurora, goddess of the dawn, is a welcome indication that the nightmarish madness of the night's events is rapidly coming to an end and that reality and sanity will return with the daylight, that 'all shall be well' (line 463) when the lovers wake up.

GLOSSARY

distracted confused, bewildered

Now take a break!

WHO SAYS ...?

1 'Not a whit. I have a device to make all well'

....

2 'What hempen homespuns have we swaggering here'

....

3 'Bless thee, Bottom! Bless thee! Thou art translated!'

....

5 'O spite! O hell! I see you are all bent / To set against me for your merriment.'

....

4 'When in that moment – so it came to pass – / Titania waked, and straightway loved an ass.'

....

ABOUT WHOM?

6 'I pray thee, gentle mortal, sing again!'

....

7 'There is no following her in this fierce vein.'

....

8 'How now, mad spirit? / What night-rule now about this haunted grove?'

....

10 'To what, my love, shall I compare thine eyne?'

....

9 'Now I but chide; but I should use thee worse, / For thou, I fear, hast given me cause to curse.'

....

Check your answers on p. 77.

SCENE 1 – Back to normal

1 Titania dotes on Bottom.

2 Oberon releases Titania from the spell so she no longer loves Bottom, and returns Bottom to his normal appearance.

3 Theseus announces that the two couples shall also be married at the wedding.

4 Bottom wakes up, thinking all the events have been a dream.

In this scene we see the significant effects of Bottom's transformation. He requests that the fairies scratch his head, and when Titania offers him delicate music and food, Bottom prefers coarse, simple music and chooses to eat dry oats, hay and dried peas – as a donkey might.

Music

References to music are important in this scene; they draw attention to harmony or discord in the relationships:

- Bottom expresses a preference for the rough and ready music of 'the tongs and the bones' (line 29). His choice creates a contrast to Titania and the fairies, whose music we know to be of a more gentle and refined nature. The contrast highlights the unsuitability of the match between them.

- Titania, on being restored by the antidote, calls for 'Music such as charmeth sleep' (line 82). This mention of delicate, soothing music reflects the harmony that has been restored.

- Theseus refers to the sound of his hounds as 'musical confusion' (line 109) and Hippolyta, remembering her hunting expedition in Crete, declares that she never heard 'So musical a discord, such sweet thunder' (line 117). The strange pleasure of a sound that is a mixture of harmony and discord is a reflection of the bitter-sweet effect of love and of the mixture of harmony and discord which has affected the events in the play. Shakespeare's use of **antithesis** matches the language to the mood, and from this scene onwards the discord gradually changes to harmony.

DID YOU KNOW?

In 1843 Mendelsshon produced some incidental music for *A Midsummer Night's Dream* – that's where the traditional 'Wedding March' comes from!

The surprise which Theseus experiences at finding the four young lovers together, with their quarrels apparently forgotten, is no greater than the surprise felt by the four young people themselves. Lysander speaks in a state 'Half sleep, half waking' (line 146) but this refers to more than that half-awake state we can all experience first thing in the morning! The nature of events in *A Midsummer Night's Dream* leave the characters unsure of what is real and what is not.

Demetrius's love for Helena is an after-effect of Oberon's spell but we accept the rightness of it because:

- He had previously loved her.

- His declaration of how much he now loves her (lines 168–75) sounds more natural than the exaggerated expressions of love in Act III, Scene 2.

- We are pleased that after all she has gone through, Helena will have the love of the man whom she loves so much.

When Bottom wakes up, all his experiences with Titania and the fairies seem to him to have been a wonderful dream. Bottom's humorous musings on the events of his 'dream' (line 204), together with his confusion over the functions of eyes and ears, make it clear that a

> **CHECKPOINT 10**
> Make a list of words which show that harmony is being restored.

> **CHECKPOINT 11**
> Who wakes up the lovers, and who is in love with whom?

DID YOU KNOW?

Bottom's words in lines 208–11 are a **parody** of a passage from the Bible: 'The eye hath not seen, and the ear hath not heard, neither have entered into the heart of man, the things which God hath prepared for them that love Him' (1 Corinthians 2:9)

simpler, more popular humour will support the play in its later stages. He plans to get Peter Quince to write a ballad about 'Bottom's Dream' (line 213) so that he can sing it as part of the play of Pyramus and Thisbe. This cleverly reminds us of how Bottom came to be involved in these strange events. It also reminds us that we still have the workmen's 'play within a play' to see, and forms a neat link with the next scene.

SCENE 2 – Bottom comes back

❶ **The workmen wonder about Bottom's whereabouts.**

❷ **Bottom returns.**

CHECKPOINT 12

How have the workmen's attitudes changed towards Bottom?

The workmen are concerned that Bottom has not returned home and that they cannot perform their play without him: 'If he come not, then the play is marred.' (line 5). The workmen's faith in Bottom's ability is rather touching. They are all convinced that Bottom would have been a great success, and Flute expresses the belief that Bottom would certainly have been well rewarded by the Duke. It is rather like a group of people talking about someone who has died; everyone tries to say something nice about him! Bottom's reappearance brings further harmony and happiness, and another bit of disorder and confusion is put right.

GLOSSARY

marred spoiled

WHO SAYS ...?

1 'Methinks I have a great desire to a bottle of hay.'

....

2 'Her dotage now I do begin to pity.'

....

3 'I wonder of their being here together.'

....

4 'It seems to me / That yet we sleep, we dream.'

....

5 'You must say "paragon". A paramour is – God bless us – a thing of naught.'

....

ABOUT WHOM?

6 'Come, sit thee down upon this flowery bed / While I thy amiable cheeks do coy.'

....

7 'But, I pray you, let none of your people stir me.'

....

8 'Now when thou wakest with thine own fool's eyes peep.'

....

9 'Tell me how it came this night / That I sleeping here was found / With these mortals on the ground.'

....

10 'Good morrow, friends – Saint Valentine is past!'

....

Check your answers on p. 77.

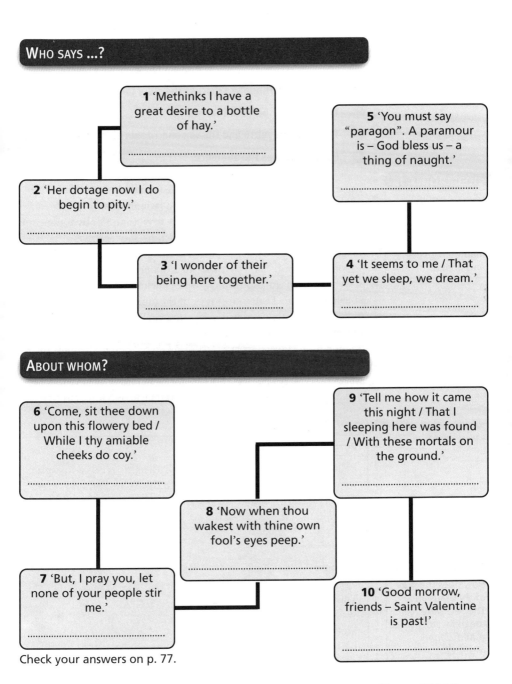

SCENE 1 – The play

1 Theseus and Hippolyta discuss the story told by the four lovers.

2 The workmen perform their play.

3 The courtiers retire and Oberon and Titania bless the marriages.

4 Puck addresses the audience.

CHECKPOINT 13

List the strange things that Theseus claims might be seen by madmen, lovers and poets.

Theseus's first speech shows he has little faith in the story the lovers tell. He dismisses stories of fairies as old fashioned and absurd, labelling them 'antique fables' and 'fairy toys' (line 3). His argument is that lovers, madmen and poets are all victims of overactive imaginations and they believe they see things that a calm, sensible person would not. Theseus is making a dramatic statement about the power of the imagination which, as he concludes, can make us mistake a bush for a bear. That same power of the imagination is vital for the audience of the play, and was even more vital for an Elizabethan audience, with so little scenery to aid imagination. Hippolyta's reaction to the lovers' story is less dismissive. Though she finds their story 'strange' (line 1), the similarities in what each of the lovers have experienced makes her feel that the stories should be believed. Shakespeare gives us both sides of the argument and leaves us to make our own decision.

Pyramus and Thisbe

Philostrate, Theseus's 'manager of mirth' (line 35), is called to explain what entertainment is available. The workmen's 'tedious brief' play (line 56) is chosen despite Philostrate's damning, but witty, description of it.

Cast\

CHECKPOINT 14

How does the play of 'Pyramus and Thisbe' relate to the main story of *A Midsummer Night's Dream*?

Prologue	Quince
Pyramus	Bottom
Thisbe	Flute
Wall	Snout
Moonshine	Starveling
Lion	Snug

- Quince enters and speaks the **Prologue**, but is so nervous that he misplaces the punctuation and so distorts the meaning of what he is trying to say.

- Quince gives a simple account of the plot while the actors perform a mime.

- Pyramus and Thisbe converse through the hole in the wall, and arrange to meet at Ninus's tomb.

- The lion and Moonshine enter.

- Thisbe enters for her meeting with Pyramus. She is frightened by the lion, and as she runs off she drops her mantle, which the lion attacks and tears with his bloodstained teeth.

- Pyramus enters. He finds the torn and bloodstained mantle. Assuming that Thisbe has been killed by the lion, Pyramus draws his sword, stabs himself, and dies.

- Thisbe returns, finds Pyramus dead, and, after what is supposed to be a tragically moving and poetic lament over his body, stabs herself.

- Having acted Pyramus' suicide, Bottom leaps up from the dead and asks whether Theseus would like the entertainment to end with an epilogue or a simple country dance known as a Bergomask.

- Theseus thanks them for their play, and asks for the dance.

 DID YOU KNOW?

Shakespeare presents us with an interesting **irony**: while Theseus condemns 'antique fables', he is himself a mythical hero whose exploits are referred to in the play.

 CHECK THE BOOK

A useful, clearly written book on Elizabethan romantic comedy is *Introducing Shakespeare* by G.B. Harrison (Penguin, 1966).

The workmen are naive, and they understand the ideas of theatre far less well than do the audience in the theatre or the courtly audience on the stage. Shakespeare uses their lack of sophistication as an important method of bringing out the **comedy** in this Act. The play of 'Pyramus and Thisbe' is crudely written in poor verse using some terrible rhymes, unnecessary repetitions, exaggerated use of **alliteration** and such ridiculous **similes** as 'His eyes were green as leeks' (line 327). The audience interrupts with witty comments on the bad acting and the action. There is even some interaction between actor and audience as Bottom replies to Theseus's comment about the wall (lines 181–4); and Starveling is clearly put out by the audience's comments. The

GLOSSARY

mirth fun, merriment

Scene 1 continued

workmen/actors are at pains to point out that what is being performed is an illusion and not any sort of reality: for example, Snug explains to the audience that he is not a real lion but only Snug the joiner.

CHECKPOINT 15

What sort of impression of night-time does Puck give in his speech? (lines 361–80)

When the actors and courtiers have retired, and Oberon and Titania have given their blessing and left the stage, Puck speaks directly to the audience. He invites the audience to regard him and the other actors as 'shadows' in a 'dream' (lines 413–28). This reminds us that, just as the characters have been bewitched and have been subject to an illusion, so we too have been involved in an illusion. His request that the audience should give him their hands is not simply an invitation to shake hands but a request that the audience should give their applause and so end the performance. The theatre audience is able to enjoy not only the workmen's comic attempt at illusion in their 'play within a play', but also the genuine illusion created by *A Midsummer Night's Dream*.

Now take a break!

WHO SAYS ...?

1 'Lovers and madmen have such seething brains'

....

6 'To the best bride bed will we, / Which by us shall blessèd be'

....

2 'For in all the play / There is not one word apt, one player fitted.'

....

5 'Sweet moon, I thank thee for thy sunny beams'

....

3 'I love not to see wretchedness o'ercharged'

....

4 'The best in this kind are but shadows; and the worst are no worse, if imagination amend them.'

....

ABOUT WHOM?

7 'Joy, gentle friends, joy and fresh days of love / Accompany your hearts.'

....

11 'This fellow doth not stand upon points.'

....

8 'Say, what abridgement have you for this evening?'

....

9 'Why, gentle sweet, you shall see no such thing.'

....

10 'My love! Thou art my love, I think?'

....

Check your answers on p. 77.

PART THREE

COMMENTARY

THEMES

LOVE

DID YOU KNOW?

Most of Shakespeare's comedies are, in one way or another, concerned with love and with the problems frequently associated with it.

Love and illusion

In this play a clear difference is drawn between the natural state of genuine love and the illusion generated by a love that has no substance. The mature love of Theseus and Hippolyta, a love forged in early conflict and adversity, is passionate – but it is also a bond between sensible and mature adults. Such a love, enshrined in marriage, should produce harmony, but when fickle lovers quarrel – as Oberon and Titania do – that quarrel will create a wider discord. The play suggests that the emotion of love needs to be balanced by reason.

Love and reason

Nothing can stand in the way of true love, even though its path may not be smooth. Hermia and Lysander are prepared to leave friends, home and family in order to be married, and Pyramus and Thisbe die for love of each other. Yet love can be a somewhat foolish thing. Doting on someone, as opposed to loving someone deeply, leads to irrational behaviour. Diana may be the goddess of the hunt, but she is also a powerful symbol of chastity, moderation and self-control. Theseus and Hippolyta, through the hunting scene in Act IV, Scene 1, are linked to her attitudes. However, Cupid, the god of love, is described by Helena as a blindfolded child irresponsibly playing tricks. The exaggerated language of those under the love-spell (that Oberon creates from the flower hit by Cupid's arrow) certainly highlights how irresponsible and irrational their behaviour is. Titania tells Bottom that she has been moved 'On the first view to say, to swear, I love thee' (III.1.134), and Lysander has declared instant love to Helena saying 'run through fire I will for thy sweet sake!' (II.2.109). It is the simple, but unbewitched, Bottom who reminds us that 'reason and love keep little company together nowadays' (III.1.136–7). Lysander's claim that his new-found love for Helena is a result of his reason is plainly ridiculous, as is Demetrius's assertion

MANCAT
COLLEGE LIBRARIES
ASHTON OLD ROAD
MANCHESTER
M11 2WH

that his heart has willingly returned 'home' to her (III.2.172). The love-juice influences the behaviour of the characters, and the idea works because we can all appreciate the fickle nature of infatuation.

CHECKPOINT 16

Whose love is affected by magic?

Love and jealousy

Love can create jealousy. The jealousy between Oberon and Titania has caused disruption and discord in the world. On a lesser level, the jealousy between the four lovers has caused such discord that Hermia and Helena abandon their lifelong friendship, betray each other and quarrel in a spiteful and abusive way, while Lysander and Demetrius develop more than a passing fancy to kill each other! When jealousy is put aside and the lovers marry, we see a return to the romantic notions of a true and lasting love.

DISCORD AND HARMONY

Closely linked to the theme of love is that of the creation of discord and harmony. The Elizabethans believed that order was a vital component in both the natural world and human life. Proper respect for lawful authority and for the order that such authority created was very important to them. There was a balance in the world, maintained by order, and when proper order was disregarded that balance was upset with terrible consequences. Shakespeare uses that idea

CHECK THE BOOK

It might be interesting to compare Shakespeare's handling of the theme of love in *A Midsummer Night's Dream* with the tragic love story of *Romeo and Juliet*.

powerfully in his play *Macbeth*, where the human chaos created by the destruction of lawful order when King Duncan is murdered is reflected by chaos, unnatural events and storms in the natural world.

In this play there are frequent quarrels, disagreements and betrayals:

- Egeus quarrels with Hermia.

- Helena betrays Hermia.

- Puck's mistake leads to misunderstandings and violent arguments between the four lovers.

- Oberon and Titania quarrel.

The discord between Oberon and Titania not only results in the destruction of crops and the misery associated with unseasonal weather, but also sets off the harmful chain of events in which the humans in this play find themselves entangled. But Oberon's decision to bewitch Titania is for a specific and limited purpose; should he succeed in gaining the boy from her then the reason for their initial quarrel will disappear. So the play is not only about discord; it is also about a progression from discord to harmony, from a state of chaos to one of order.

Use of music

We usually associate the words discord and harmony with music, and there are several occasions in the play when music, singing and dancing are all used to introduce a note of happiness. Music is used, or mentioned, frequently in scenes involving the fairies and you might have noticed that in the latter part of the play, as the plot moves from chaos/disorder towards order/harmony, the musical interludes are more frequent.

AGE AND YOUTH

Strict father and wilful daughter

The differences in attitude between young and old are first shown in the behaviour of Egeus and his daughter, Hermia. Egeus feels he has the right to insist on directing the course of Hermia's life irrespective of her own wishes and feelings. He has the law – the idea of good

CHECKPOINT 17

Consider the occasions when music is mentioned or used, and the effect that the music creates.

order – on his side, and he dismisses her reluctance as evidence of stubbornness brought on by Lysander's cunning manipulation of her youth and inexperience. The tricks that Lysander is accused of using were simply the writing of love poems, singing of love songs and giving of small presents as tokens of his love. All of these things were quite normal ways for an Elizabethan gentleman to show his love for the lady of his choice. They may not be exactly what a young man might do today, but we can all recognise something similar in modern relationships. The reactions of Hermia and Lysander to what Egeus and Theseus say to them indicate their love is genuine, but Egeus sees it as insincere and accuses Lysander of 'feigning love' (I.1.31).

Theseus – a symbol of age and order

Though Theseus is more mature than Hermia and Lysander, he is newly in love and so has considerable sympathy for them. His status as the upholder of the law, however, puts him in a difficult position. While he is prepared to spare Hermia from death, he is not, at the beginning of the play, prepared to set aside her father's rights under the law. Later on, when he sees that the lovers have resolved their differences so that Demetrius no longer wishes to make any claim on Hermia, Theseus is able to change sides and allow his sympathy with the young to overrule his sense of duty to the old.

The youngsters

While Theseus might be able to see both sides of the argument, we are in little doubt that the young will not see things through the eyes of the old. They will not 'choose love by another's eyes' (I.1.140) and Egeus is unlikely to comply with Hermia's desire that 'I would my father looked but with my eyes' (I.1.56). The generations would not see eye to eye and Hermia's determination to become a nun, or even to be put to death, rather than marry a man she does not love strikes a sympathetic chord. We feel that Egeus and the older generation surround themselves with attitudes that restrict the freedom that the younger generation desperately seeks.

CLASSICAL MYTHOLOGY

We must be careful not to think that this play is actually about classical (ancient Greek and Roman) mythology. The references to

GLOSSARY

feigning faking/pretending

DID YOU KNOW?
Ancient beliefs in a variety of gods are a rich source of ideas for Shakespeare's plays.

characters from mythology help to set the scene and provide useful reference points. The Elizabethan audience would have been more familiar with mythological characters than most people today.

Theseus and Hippolyta

Theseus and Hippolyta feature in Greek legend. Theseus was famed for his bravery. He captured the fire-breathing bull of Marathon, slew the Minotaur and helped to defeat the Centaurs – creatures that were half man and half horse. It was in his defence of Athens against the invading Amazons, a tribe of fierce female warriors, that he met and fell in love with the Amazon Queen, Hippolyta. Theseus and Hippolyta make a useful example of mature love against which to set the chaotic events generated by Oberon's use of the love-juice.

Mention is made of the ancient cities of Athens, Sparta and Thebes and the region of Thessaly. There are also references to mythological heroes and lovers. Among these are Corin and Phillida. Titania accuses Oberon of disguising himself as Corin in order to flirt with Phillida. Oberon responds by dragging up Titania's affection for Theseus, while reminding Titania of Perigeria, Aegles, Ariadne and Antiopa – all of whom were former lovers of Theseus. The play of 'Pyramus and Thisbe' is based on those two Babylonian lovers. Pyramus and Thisbe meet at the tomb of Ninus, who was the founder of Ninevah. As with the references to gods and goddesses, some of these references help to create images that boost the impact of the events taking place. They also set the events within a clear context, but more importantly they add an essentially mysterious, unreal, dream-like quality to the events.

NIGHT–TIME

For many scenes, the darkness brought by night is an essential ingredient. Night is when humans usually sleep and when magical beings are about. We do not see very well in the dark, and that physical inability to see clearly is a parallel to the inability to understand when we are confused. While the fairies feel at home in the dark, the human characters do not. They become lost and frightened. As Oberon and Puck manipulate their emotions, the humans lose their true identities, seeming to change their appearance, attitudes and affections from scene to scene. Shakespeare uses the contrast between

Greek and Roman deities

In the play there are references to many Greek (and Roman) gods and goddesses:

- Diana was the Roman goddess of the moon, hunting and chastity. Shakespeare also refers to her by her other name, Phoebe.

- Venus was the goddess of love, and Cupid the child-like god whose arrows pierced the heart to cause the 'victims' to fall in love.

- Apollo was the god of the sun, also known as Phoebus (whom Bottom mistakenly calls 'Phibbus').

- Hecate, a mysterious goddess with influence over heaven, earth and hell, was usually portrayed as having three heads. She was regarded as an evil deity and was thought to command the evil spirits.

- Bacchus was the god of wine.

- Neptune, or Poseidon, was the god of the sea.

- Aurora was the goddess of the dawn.

- The Fates were three sisters who controlled each man's birth, life and death.

- The Furies were the three goddesses who punished all wrongdoers.

These references are all used in the play to indicate forces that are outside human control yet influence aspects of human life.

DID YOU KNOW?

Robert Greene, an older, more experienced writer, jealously described Shakespeare as 'an upstart crow' who thought of himself as the 'only Shake-scene' in the country.

daylight and darkness, and the importance of being able to see clearly and to believe what we see, to reflect the states of knowledge and ignorance through which the characters pass. For much of the play they do not know or understand what is going on – they are 'in the dark'; with the daylight comes the revelation of a kind of truth, an ability to see, and an inclination to put their trust in what they see. No longer are bushes seen as bears.

THE MOON

CHECKPOINT 18

Look for the different occasions when the moon is mentioned.

The moon and its light figure prominently in the play. Moonlight is very different from daylight, and the moonlight creates a magical and mysterious world in which natural forms are disguised. The full moon was said to affect people's behaviour, to make them mad. Indeed the word 'lunatic' stems from the Latin for 'moon'. The behaviour of the characters during the moonlit scenes is unnatural and irrational.

At the beginning of the play the moon is described as 'like to a silver bow / New-bent in heaven' (I.1.9–10). This powerful image of a weapon ready to fire its destructive missile at the world is an apt way of introducing the madness that will follow.

THE NATURAL WORLD

The world of nature is, in this play, shown as being a place of great beauty and an area of potential danger. The place where Titania sleeps is an enchanting bower where fragrant flowers grow. Yet it is in the woods, a wild place, where Bottom and the lovers can feel lost and afraid. The woods are a place of mystery and magic, closely associated with the fairies. They are also a place where snakes, spiders, beetles, bats and other creatures, believed to be or actually dangerous, can threaten the peace of even one so powerful as Titania. Oberon speaks of such fearsome creatures as lions, bears and wolves – creatures that can be hunted in daylight by Theseus and his hounds but which would present real danger at night. Nature is full of life and anyone who is familiar with the countryside will know that there you are surrounded by vast numbers of creatures of assorted shapes and sizes even when you cannot see them. Nature helps us to survive, to grow our crops and to feed our animals, but it can also be cruel, unpredictable and destructive.

DID YOU KNOW?
Elizabethans were very conscious of the parallels between human life and the natural world.

The colours Shakespeare mentions – from the cold, pale light of the moon which distorts and confuses, to the fiery red glow of the dawn which warms and comforts – affect our feelings and perceptions. The colours of ravens and doves, spotted snakes with enamelled skins, milk-white and purple flowers, even the 'cherry nose' and 'yellow cowslip cheeks' of Pyramus (V.1.323–4), all create images and enhance contrasts. The way that the natural world can be harmonious and balanced is an example to the human world; but just as the human world can suffer discord and unrest, so too the natural world can be unbalanced and dangerous.

IMAGINATION AND ILLUSION

Every play depends upon creating an illusion with the help of the imagination of the audience. A well-worked illusion can seem real. In this play there is confusion among the characters as to what is real and what is not. They spend their time in a dream-like state where reason is clouded and they are no longer sure of themselves or of the reality they think they see. It is interesting to notice how often characters sleep in this play. When we sleep we frequently experience dreams that seem so real to us that we can wake confused or frightened. Shakespeare uses sleep as a convenient way to enable Oberon to cast his spells and either to create or to sort out problems. Yet when the characters wake, their ideas of what is real are changed, and they have the same confusion that we might experience through having a dream. That confusion is heightened because the reality that they are experiencing has also changed – they fall in and out of love or they grow monstrous heads!

Oberon creates the illusion of love, and the belief that Lysander and Demetrius have in that illusory love causes chaos. Puck disguises

GLOSSARY
cowslip primrose

CHECKPOINT 19

Consider the range of illusions that are presented to us during the play.

himself and creates the illusions that the workmen are being chased by wild creatures or that Demetrius and Lysander are chasing each other when they are really following Puck's voice. We, the audience, can smile at these illusions, as we can at the workmen's attempts to create an illusion through their play of 'Pyramus and Thisbe'. Yet we too are involved in the illusion that is theatre, for while we watch the characters being tricked, we easily lose sight of the fact that those characters only live because we let them live in our imaginations.

STRUCTURE

In his plays Shakespeare normally has a central plot beneath which we can find one, or more, sub-plot. It is usually quite easy to recognise the main plot and to see how the sub-plots fit in with it. In *A Midsummer Night's Dream*, however, we have three quite distinct groups of characters whose activities form four plots of more or less equal importance.

The three groups of characters:
❶ the courtiers
❷ the workmen
❸ the fairies

The four plots:
❶ The wedding of Theseus and Hippolyta
❷ The tangled love affairs between Hermia, Lysander, Demetrius and Helena
❸ The workmen's planning, rehearsal and performance of the play 'Pyramus and Thisbe'
❹ The quarrel between Oberon and Titania (which gives rise to the fairies' plot)

Each of these four strands of the play inevitably crosses and links with each of the others as the groups come into contact with one other, knowingly or unknowingly. Shakespeare makes full use of the possibilities opened up by the very different kinds of characters within each group and the different dramatic opportunities offered by the situations in which they are involved. The groups contrast vividly: the sophisticated, yet earth-bound, regal splendour of Theseus and Hippolyta; the homespun vulgarity of Bottom and the workmen; the ephemeral delicacy of the fairies. The changes in mood as each group takes centre stage, and the contrasts when their worlds meet, give each scene a subtly different atmosphere.

The action of the play is divided by time and location. According to the opening lines, there are four days from the start of the play to the wedding day, though in fact there are only three clearly distinguishable days. The error need not bother us unduly since it makes no difference to the action or to our understanding of the events. The opening scene is in daylight, as is the latter part of Act IV, Scene 1 when Theseus wakes the four lovers. Theseus embodies the ideas of maturity, stability and reason and these qualities thrive in the light when things are seen clearly. The main body of the action takes place in the darkness of a wood at night. Unlike the wakeful clarity of the daylight scenes, these woodland scenes contain impish mischief, immature behaviour, irrational actions and confusion.

CHECK THE FILM

The Royal Shakespeare Company produced a version of *A Midsummer Night's Dream* in 1968.

Although it is clearly a comedy, the play contains elements which suggest potential danger or tragedy. At the very start of the play we are reminded of the previous conflict between Theseus and Hippolyta. The argument between Egeus and Hermia immediately shows up the rifts in family life. Helena betrays her close friend and the conflict that is created between the four lovers leads to threats and violent quarrels. Yet we are kept aware that all these potentially harmful situations are being observed, monitored and controlled. Oberon ensures that Puck will keep Lysander and Demetrius apart and that each lover will end up with the right partner. The quarrel between Oberon and Titania is used as a springboard for the tangled chain of events that follows. Yet even that quarrel, which has such terrible consequences for humankind, leads not to bloodshed but to the ridiculously funny situation of Titania falling in love with ass-headed Bottom. So the play has progressed from the happy thoughts of the royal wedding to a series of conflicts and confusions. All conflicts which have flourished in the night are resolved harmoniously by the time dawn breaks.

CHECKPOINT 20

Aside from the farcical performance, does 'Pyramus and Thisbe' remind you of any other Shakespeare play?

These conflicts are not out of place in comedy. Drama needs to reflect life, and conflict is an integral part of life. When everything is resolved and we have a happy ending, the earlier conflicts make that happiness more complete.

The workmen's performance of 'Pyramus and Thisbe' brings an element of **farce** to round off the proceedings. Their play is based on a tragic subject, but their inept performance creates a humorous response which removes any tragic effect. Rather as in *A Midsummer Night's Dream*, the potential for tragedy never becomes a reality, and the good humour at the start of the play is restored and increased. To emphasise the happiness of the ending, the fairies arrive to bless and protect the newly-weds.

The play's tangled structure creates the atmosphere of a dream, and in a sense that is what all theatre does – presents us with an illusion that we temporarily see as reality.

CHARACTERS

THESEUS

Regal
Kind
Passionate
Practical

Theseus, in Greek legend, was a great hero and a brave warrior, who did a great deal to improve the way that Greek society worked, giving each citizen responsibilities and duties, as well as rights. In the play, he is presented as a good example of what a sixteenth-century ruler should be. He is strong and heroic; he is aware of his responsibility for maintaining good order and upholding the law; he is thoughtful when making decisions and approaches his duties in a kindly way; he supports the arts and is also a keen sportsman.

In his dealings with Egeus and Hermia we see his firmness in upholding Egeus's rights under the law, but we also see how his suggestion of a lesser penalty than death offers Hermia some hope and calms a dangerous situation. Later in the play, when it is clear that Demetrius no longer wants to marry Hermia, Theseus allows his common sense to dictate his actions. Again, he calms the situation and seems, after the chaos and irrationality of the night, to be the voice of reason that restores order to the events. His decision that the four young lovers may marry the partners of their choice is also an indication of the influence that his love for Hippolyta has had upon him. Despite his rather sceptical dismissal of the overactive imaginations of lovers, whom he groups with poets and madmen (V.1.7), it is clear that Theseus is himself somewhat romantic and passionate. His impatience for his wedding to Hippolyta, the various terms of endearment that he uses towards her – and the list of his former lovers – show that other side to his character. His kindness is revealed early on in the play when he shows sympathy towards Hermia and seems prepared to take Egeus aside for a calm discussion of the situation. Later in the play, that same quality is evident in the generous attitude he has towards the well-intentioned efforts of his subjects, especially the workmen's inept production of a play. He joins in the humorous remarks of the courtiers, but his humour is gentle and his thanks to the men at the end of the play are sincere.

In the course of the play, Theseus performs a number of important functions. He is the upholder of the law, a reasoning and flexible spokesman for calm and common sense, a restorer of balance and fairness and a defender of honest effort.

HIPPOLYTA

Hippolyta is herself a heroic character. She was the queen of the Amazons, defeated in battle by Theseus. In some versions of the myth she was ravaged by Theseus and ran away from him, but in other versions they married and lived happily. It is not surprising that Shakespeare chose the happier version! Her qualities of kindness, bravery, regal bearing, good humour and obedience to a higher authority suit her for the role as it would have been seen by an Elizabethan audience.

With Theseus, Hippolyta represents a more mature form of love than the impulsive, youthful romanticism of the four lovers. She is more reconciled to waiting for the wedding day than Theseus is. She has rather more sympathy for the story told by the lovers. Her sensitivity, insight and natural warmth lead her to think that their tale is something more than a figment of the imagination.

Brave
Thoughtful
Loving
Humorous

Those same qualities affect her reaction to the proposal that the court should see the workmen's play. She is concerned that they will make fools of themselves because she does not really believe that they are capable of anything so ambitious. As she watches their play she says 'This is the silliest stuff that ever I heard' (V.1.208), yet her humorous comments are, like those of Theseus, gentle, and she is quick to offer Moonshine some praise when his distress at the interruptions becomes clear.

THE LOVERS

While we need to consider each of the four young lovers as individuals, we can also see that they work dramatically as a group. They represent a more romantic, volatile and passionate side of love than that we see in Theseus and Hippolyta. Some people feel that these four characters lack depth, and that they are, therefore, easily confused with each other. They certainly do share several characteristics. The girls are both romantic, both dote on the man of their choice, both become confused and argumentative. The two young men both become victims of an illusion of love, both turn their backs on the girl they have once loved, both fight for Hermia and then for Helena, both speak in a similarly exaggerated romantic way. For the purposes of this play such similarities are no real problem. Yes, they can lead to confusion, but the four lovers is a symbol of young love and their language is that of Elizabethan love poetry. In this way they are quite an effective way for Shakespeare to present his theme of young love, a theme that does not depend upon individuals.

HERMIA

We learn that Hermia has dark hair, that she is shorter than Helena and that she is regarded as being beautiful. The name Hermia is derived from Hermes, the messenger of the gods, who was also known as Mercury. The name is appropriate as a **characternym** since she changes mood quickly and so she is a 'mercurial' character. She is the first of the four lovers to come to our attention. We see her in dispute with her father, who considers her to be disobedient and wilful, with a 'stubborn harshness' (I.1.38). Many people today can readily sympathise with her disobedience and with her decision to run away from Athens in order to marry Lysander. To the Elizabethans,

Short
Dark
Passionate
Stubborn

however, such disobedient and reckless behaviour would have been a cause for great disapproval.

In the woods, Hermia shows modesty in not allowing Lysander to lie down too closely to her. She shows considerable spirit in her verbal attack on Demetrius when she thinks he has killed Lysander, and that spirit is again evident in her fury at what she sees as Helena's underhanded plot to steal Lysander from her. This spirit is an echo of the defiance and self-confidence we have seen in her stand against her father and in her willingness to run away with Lysander. As an audience we see her fury in the woods as amusing, especially when she bases her attack on Helena on a belief that it is the difference in their height that has led Lysander to love Helena.

HELENA

Helena's name perhaps reminds us of Helen of Troy, the beautiful woman whose abduction started the ten-year Trojan War. The name means 'light', and this is appropriate since she has a fair complexion and is supposed to be regarded as being as beautiful as Hermia. Unlike Hermia, Helena is rather timid. She lacks Hermia's self-confidence, which is understandable since she has been wooed and then rejected by Demetrius. She dotes on Demetrius so much that she is willing to betray her best friend's secret and to follow Demetrius into the woods. She begs him 'Use me but as your spaniel' (II.1.205), and to beat her rather than to ignore her. Her loyalty to Demetrius never really changes. She suffers confusion and pain when she thinks that the other three are making fun of her and this makes her somewhat more vulnerable and sympathetic than Hermia. It is worth considering how you feel about her happiness at the end of the play. She has got back her lover, Demetrius, but he is still under the influence of Oberon's spell so that, unlike Hermia who has a true love, Helena is left only with a love that is a sort of illusion. Does that make her an object of ridicule or one of sympathy?

Tall
Fair
Loving
Timid

LYSANDER

The account that Egeus gives of how Lysander had 'stolen' Hermia's affections (I.1.26–38) shows us that Lysander is a romantic person whose approach to Hermia has been sensitive and determined. He is a wealthy

young man whose witty comments during the performance of 'Pyramus and Thisbe' show him to be at home in the refined atmosphere of the court. If it were not for Egeus's unexplained dislike of him, he would seem a most eligible suitor. He shows no fear of Egeus, or of Theseus. He states his case in a forthright and outspoken manner and he is not slow to point out the poor behaviour of Demetrius, who has led Helena on and then dropped her for Hermia. Lysander is keen to make it clear that he is faithful in his love – though we know that future events will temporarily change this. His disdain for Demetrius is shown early on when he says that since Demetrius has the love of Egeus, Demetrius should marry him and leave Hermia to Lysander. That disdain continues in their various meetings in the woods. The two men are reconciled at the end of the play, but not before Lysander has accepted the blustering challenge that Demetrius has made.

Romantic
Outspoken
Passionate
Witty

Lysander's loving nature and his romantic plan to elope tend to put us on his side. When he is under the influence of the love-juice, his hateful contempt for the devoted Hermia seems all the more cruel, but it is a useful reminder of how easily the affections of the young can be swayed.

DEMETRIUS

Demetrius is a rather less likeable character than is Lysander. Though he has the support of Egeus, the revelation that he has previously expressed his love for Helena and has now rejected her makes us agree with Lysander that he is an 'inconstant man' (I.1.110) and has behaved badly. Unlike Lysander, Demetrius is not a faithful lover. It is interesting that Theseus should want to talk to him as well as to Egeus at the end of the first scene. The negative view that we have of him is deepened by his treatment of Helena. Far from being grateful to her for the information about Hermia's elopement, he treats Helena badly. He abuses her and threatens her so that we find him callous, selfish and uncaring, and Helena tells him as much: 'you hard-hearted adamant!' (II.1.195)

Self-centred
Hot-headed
Deceitful
Cruel

In the first part of the play Demetrius appears somewhat serious and certainly unattractive. His emotions in the woods seem to stem from a sense of being thwarted rather than from a genuine love of Hermia.

When he is bewitched and falls in love with Helena the unreal nature of that love is reflected in the exaggerated nature of his language. He does become a figure of fun, and by the end of the play is a much more sympathetic character who, like Lysander, amuses us with his witty comments on the workmen's performance of their play.

It is as well to remember that Demetrius remains under the influence of the love-juice, so that his love for Helena is not a natural love but one that has been forced upon him. Similarly we could think that his more jovial nature is a side-effect of the spell. Whether we think it fair on Helena and Demetrius that his love is really an illusion, it does seem that they are happy, and we might well consider that Oberon has done them a favour in giving them some sort of happiness. If we do feel that, it is probably more because we want Helena to be happy than out of any desire that Demetrius should feel like that!

EGEUS

Hermia's father is rather narrow-minded. He has an authoritarian view of his position as a father, insisting on the 'obedience that is due to me' (I.1.37). He has little sympathy for young love. His demand for the harshest penalty of the law – death for his disobedient daughter – seems cruel and unnatural. He is not a strongly-drawn character, but he represents an older generation that contrasts with the exuberant and more wilful younger generation. Dramatically he provides a springboard for the elopement and for all the events in which the four young lovers become involved.

Old
Stern
Narrow-minded
Determined

BOTTOM

Bottom is a weaver by trade, and there are several references to that trade in the play. He is far more developed as a character than the other workmen, and so may be considered in greater detail. He is a boisterous character who is full of enthusiasm and self-confidence when he is with his fellow workers. That self-confidence suffers a set-back when the others run away from him, but it returns quickly when Titania expresses her love and the fairies show him such attention. It is that same self-confidence that lets him believe in his ability as an actor and that leads him to correct Theseus's comment on what might

GLOSSARY
inconstant fickle
adamant very hard stone

happen next in the workmen's performance of 'Pyramus and Thisbe'. As the central character among the workmen he links their activities with the world of the court and with the world of the fairies.

Bottom is a thoroughly honest, if sometimes misguided, character. He is a simple man and that simplicity is apparent in the contrast between himself and the majestic Titania. The pleasure he feels at the attention he receives from the fairies is touching, as is the politeness with which he conducts himself.

The other workmen regard him highly. They listen to his suggestions, they are impressed by what they see as his considerable acting ability, they refer to him as 'Bully Bottom' (III.1.7) which is a term of endearment and they believe he has 'the best wit of any handicraft man in Athens' (IV.2.9–10). Bottom is at the centre of the funniest scenes in the play. When he wakes up after his experiences with Titania he finds it difficult to separate reality from illusion. This is just what he does when they are rehearsing and performing their play. His comment that he will get Quince to write the story and call it 'Bottom's Dream' (IV.1.213) perhaps reflects Shakespeare's awareness that many people will see Bottom as the central figure of the play. Whether you will be one of those people by the time you have finished considering all aspects of the play remains to be seen.

Energetic
Simple
Honest
Friendly

THE OTHER WORKMEN

These may be considered as a group. They are simple men, and their simplicity is reflected by the descriptions of them as 'hempen homespuns' (III.1.70), 'rude mechanicals' (III.2.9), 'Hard-handed men' (V.1.72), who are 'clowns' (see the stage directions at the beginning of Act III, Scene 1) dismissed by Puck as being of 'that barren sort' (III.2.13). Despite these unflattering descriptions, as a group they represent honest toil, decency, loyalty and endeavour. We are amused by their antics and by their naivety, but we are intended to share Theseus's view that they are worthy of praise because their intentions are good and their efforts are sincere.

Names and trades

Each of the men is identified by a name and a trade, and each has something that makes him different from the others:

- PETER QUINCE: a carpenter, also the one who has written the play and who is trying to organise the rehearsals. Quines or quince was the name given to blocks of wood, but a quince is also a fruit, noted for its sharp taste, which was popularly used for making jam: Peter Quince behaves at times in a sharp way and his attempts to put on a play could also be said to land the workmen in a jam! Although he becomes a little irritated by Bottom's attempts to run things, he generally remains tolerant. His flattering reasons why Bottom must play the part of Pyramus are a good example of his tact.

- FRANCIS FLUTE: the bellows-mender, and like a bellows a flute is something that works by a sort of wind power. Wind is insubstantial, and really so is Francis Flute. He is quite a young man. It is natural that he should be chosen to play the part of Thisbe, but as he is proud of the fact 'I have a beard coming' (I.2.43–4), we can understand his reluctance to shave it off and play the part of a woman.

- TOM SNOUT: a tinker, that is someone who mends pots and pans; part of a pot would have been the spout or snout. At first he is asked to take the part of Pyramus's father, but the workmen's concerns over making the wall seem real mean that he ends up playing Wall.

- SNUG: a joiner, so would be expected to make the wooden joints fit snugly. He describes himself as 'slow of study' (I.2.63) and Quince may have recognised that fact by casting Snug as the lion, a part that required no lines to be learned.

- ROBIN STARVELING: a tailor. Tailors were caricatured as being miserly and prepared to rob their customers by charging them for more cloth than they had actually used. He is cast as Thisbe's mother, but his part is changed to that of Moonshine as a result of the men's concern for making the play seem real. Starveling is considerably put out by the interruptions that occur during their performance.

 DID YOU KNOW?

The National Portrait Gallery in London has some excellent paintings which clearly show how the Elizabethans loved to display their wealth and status through their beautiful, bejewelled and richly decorated clothes – and that is just the men!

OBERON

As the King of the Fairies, Oberon represents power in his world in much the same way that Theseus does in the human world. Oberon, however, uses his power rather differently. He is more volatile, and his first words, 'Ill met by moonlight, proud Titania!' (II.1.60), are a stark contrast to Theseus's words of love. While Theseus is a thoughtful, rational ruler who brings a sense of order and calm, Oberon is a creator of dreams, someone who works in the realms of imagination and whose mischievous use of power brings chaos and confusion.

Oberon is very much a creature of the night. There is a darkness to his character which can make him rather frightening. He is jealous of Titania because she has the boy and he wants the boy for his page. His jealousy has caused havoc in nature and his plan to get the boy involves making a fool of Titania. He is a creature of contradictions. We see that he expects to get his own way and that he is prepared to be ruthless in his use of mysterious powers to ensure that he gets what he wants. Yet he is capable of feeling sympathy and compassion. He releases Titania from the spell as soon as his objective is accomplished, and it is his sympathy for Helena's treatment by Demetrius that leads him to act on her behalf. He can create a spell which has the potential to harm Titania, yet he can also cast a spell that will protect an unborn child from harm.

Oberon has considerable powers. He can see what others, even Puck, cannot and he has observed the gods going about their business. He has a deep knowledge and understanding of the workings of the powers of herbs and plants and of nature. When he describes the mermaid riding on a dolphin's back, the movement of the sea, and the change that gave the flower 'love in idleness' (II.1.168) its powers, we recognise that he is so close to nature that he seems a part of it. Oberon displays certain human traits; he is capable of jealousy, anger, pity and mischief. But while he may influence events in the world of men he is not a part of that world. He is a dream figure whose strange combination of goodness and mischief, compassion and vengeance is as magical as his power. The power of that magic is reflected in the power of the language that he uses.

Imperious
Influential
Magical
Jealous
Mischievous

TITANIA

Titania is the Queen of the Fairies. Oberon describes her as 'proud' (II.1.60) because she has refused to agree to his demand to hand over the Indian boy. Her reasons, however, seem to make some sense, and they suggest that she wants to protect the boy in order to repay the loyalty that the boy's mother had displayed. She is prepared to stand up to Oberon. When he chides her with 'Tarry, rash wanton! Am I not thy lord?', she responds rather ambiguously with 'Then I must be thy lady' (II.1.63–4). Oberon's language can be moving and magical, and Titania's language is beautifully poetic. There is an underlying sensuality in the poetry of her language, and she is a passionate creature who expresses her emotions in a physical way. The intimacy with which she treats Bottom highlights the sensual side of her nature, but the scenes with Bottom also highlight the difference between his 'mortal grossness' (III.1.151) and her delicate beauty.

- Regal
- Proud
- Beautiful
- Caring

Titania's quarrel with Oberon has caused destruction in nature, and Titania's comments about the natural beauty of the world suggest she is in touch with nature and with its beauty. She sends her fairies to improve the appearance of plants and flowers, and to fight against unpleasant creatures. Under the spell of the love-juice she degrades herself by her devotion to Bottom, but because Bottom is himself such a likeable character there is no real harm done. We are pleased when her senses are restored and when the quarrel between herself and Oberon is resolved. The 'amity' and affection that these two show at the end of the play once again shows how a love that has come through a time of adversity is perhaps a stronger, richer love.

PUCK

Strictly speaking the character is Robin Goodfellow, who is a puck, an impish spirit from English folklore. He has none of the dignity of Titania or Oberon, and from our first meeting with him we realise that he delights in mischief and trickery: he is indeed a 'knavish sprite' (II.1.33). Puck steers clear of emotional entanglements, unlike all the other main characters, who become deeply involved in each other's lives. He simply enjoys creating the circumstances in which ridiculous events and behaviour are inevitable. He sometimes acts under the direct instructions of his master, Oberon, but there are suggestions

GLOSSARY

Tarry wait

wanton sexually promiscuous woman

amity friendliness

Mischievous
Loyal to Oberon

that he has an independent mind. Oberon himself says that perhaps Puck 'committest thy knaveries wilfully' (III.2.346), and the trick of putting an ass's head on Bottom was certainly Puck's own idea.

Puck loves practical jokes. In Act II, Scene 1 we have descriptions of some of his jokes. He is a powerful creature who can 'put a girdle round about the earth / In forty minutes!' (II.1.175–6), can change his appearance and voice and can perform dramatic transformations of living creatures. While he claims that 'those things do best please me / That befall preposterously' (III.2.120–21) we might find it hard to really like Puck or to fully share his pleasure in his tricks because, unlike Oberon, he lacks any feelings of compassion. His loyalty to Oberon is, however, beyond question, and when he mistakes Lysander for Demetrius it is an honest mistake. Although Puck is certainly irresponsible, the control that Oberon exercises means that Puck is not only instrumental in causing the chaos and confusion among the four human lovers, but also instrumental in protecting them from real harm and finally bringing them to a happy state of harmony.

CHECK THE FILM
The 1999 version of *A Midsummer Night's Dream* boasts an all-star cast, including Kevin Kline as Bottom and Michelle Pfeiffer as Titania.

THE FAIRIES

Peaseblossom, Cobweb, Moth and Mustardseed are the four fairies mentioned by name. They are loyal followers of Titania who obey her wishes and spend their time helping Nature. Their names are all taken from natural objects. They are attentive to Bottom, though they must see what a ridiculous creature he is.

LANGUAGE AND STYLE

Shakespeare's use of language gives us real clues about who is speaking and about what is happening. Language was of major importance during the time in which Shakespeare was writing. Actors in Elizabethan times relied upon the delivery of the words, rather than on the use of gestures or facial expressions, to bring out the characters they were playing. The action of the play, as well as its attraction, was to be found in the flow of the language.

The sort of language that Shakespeare uses is a strong indication of the themes of the play as well as of the characters:

- BLANK VERSE: The language of the courtiers, Theseus, Hippolyta, Oberon and Titania, shows their high status.

- PROSE: The language of Bottom and the workmen, reflects their low status.

- POETIC VERSE: The play of *Pyramus and Thisbe* is written in poor quality verse with rather a sing-song rhythm. Verse which should signify the aristocratic nature of Pyramus and Thisbe actually emphasises that the workmen are pretending to be what they are not.

METRE

The high-status characters such as the courtiers speak mainly in **unrhymed iambic pentameter**, or blank verse. Each line contains ten syllables divided into five pairs of syllables. The word 'iambic' tells us that these pairs of syllables, or 'feet', each consist of an unstressed syllable followed by a stressed syllable. You will, however, notice that there are many variations to this and that few of the lines conform completely to this rigid structure. There are many reasons for this. Sometimes Shakespeare might want to emphasise a particular word and the change in stress pattern helps him to do this. At other times you will notice that one character's speech ends on a short line and that the next character's speech begins with another short line. This can indicate, for example, two sides to a quarrel: where Hermia responds to Theseus' observation that 'Demetrius is a worthy gentleman' (I.1.52) we have:

HERMIA   So is Lysander.

THESEUS   In himself he is;
           But in this kind, wanting your father's voice,
           The other must be held the worthier.

                               (I.1.53–5)

This same device can indicate two characters working closely together: when Puck returns with the flower, we have:

PUCK   Ay, there it is.

OBERON   I pray thee give it me.

                               (II.1.248)

CHECK THE BOOK
As well as using verse forms in many of his plays, Shakespeare wrote poetry for its own sake. As a poet he is perhaps best known for his Sonnets which were published in 1609.

We must also realise that an entire play written in perfectly rhythmical and unrhymed pentameters would be rather tedious! Early on when Hermia and Lysander are alone and discussing their love for each other, Shakespeare introduces **rhyming couplets** that add a more romantic note (I.1.171–251). The simple couplet form accentuates the innocence as well as the love of these two. When Titania uses rhyming couplets in her expressions of love for Bottom, those rhymes emphasise Titania's delicate and sensuous nature. By contrast the rhymes used by Lysander (Act 2, Scene 2) and by Demetrius (Act 3, Scene 2) to express love for Helena are so extravagant that they emphasise the lack of substance that exists in the illusion of love.

LITERARY DEVICES

Shakespeare's language can, at times, seem almost overloaded with literary devices:

CHECK THE FILM

An animated version of *A Midsummer Night's Dream* was produced for the BBC series 'Shakespeare – The Animated Tales'. This animated version was directed by Robert Saakiants.

- PUNS: such as in the somewhat crude link between Bottom's name and the head of an ass and in Demetrius' assertion that he is 'wood within this wood' (II.1.192)

- ANTITHESIS: as when Helena says she will 'make a heaven of hell' (II.1.243), and in Act 5, Scene 1 when Theseus reads out the description of the workmen's play

- METAPHOR: as when Lysander refers to Hermia as a 'tawny Tartar', a 'cat' and a 'serpent' (III.2.260–63), while Hermia retaliates by accusing Helena of being a 'juggler', a 'canker-blossom' and a 'thief of love' (III.2.282–3)

- ALLITERATION: in such lines as Theseus' instruction to Hermia: 'fit your fancies to your father's will' (1.1.118); and, much more comically, in Quince's **Prologue** when he says:

> 'Whereat with blade – with bloody, blameful blade –
> He bravely broached his boiling bloody breast.'

(V.1.145–6)

ATMOSPHERE

The overall atmosphere of the play is a magical one, which Shakespeare creates by a mixture of the real world with a mythical one. He uses the verse to create the atmosphere of each scene. Our understanding of this is made stronger when we recognise the changing moods of the characters. A good way to think about what mood is being created is to consider what tone of voice the characters might adopt.

There are times, such as in Act I, Scene 1, when Theseus speaks in a weighty, serious way, but when he discovers the four sleeping lovers the atmosphere is much lighter. This is seen in the gently mocking tone of his words that suggests the light-hearted mood Shakespeare wants to create.

CHECK THE BOOK

A light-hearted view of the Elizabethan period may be found in the irreverent historical account *The Terrible Tudors* by Terry Deary and Neil Tongue (Scholastic, 1993).

IMAGERY

Much of the **imagery** comes from the many references to Greek gods, goddesses and heroes. We have, for example, mention of:

- Cupid, who represents love

- Diana, who represents chastity

- Aurora, who brings the new dawn

- The battle with the Centaurs

- The Bacchanalian orgy at which Orpheus was torn to pieces

There are also plenty of references to nature, to native beasts, birds and flowers:

- The 'bank where the wild thyme blows' and the 'luscious woodbine' (II.1.249–51) create an atmosphere which suits the heady, exotic and sensual world of the fairies.

- Titania mentions the 'crimson rose' filled with 'hoary-headed frosts' (II.1.107–8) and calls for musk-roses to put in Bottom's mane (IV.1.3).

- Titania's image of honeysuckle and ivy twined round the elm (IV.1.41–3) conjures up the image of Titania herself entwined round Bottom.

- Fruits are mentioned: 'apricocks, dewberries, grapes, figs and mulberries' (III.1.161–2).

DID YOU KNOW?
The comedic nature of *A Midsummer Night's Dream* was not appreciated by Samuel Pepys, who described it as 'the most insipid and ridiculous play that ever I saw in my life' (diary, 1662).

- We are reminded of a host of less pleasant images in Act 3, Scene 2: spiders, beetles, blind worms (slow worms) snails and worms (snakes).

- A serpent skin can protect a sleeping fairy (II.1.255–6), but in her dream a serpent also eats Hermia's heart (II.2.151–6).

- Bottom sings of the ousel cock (blackbird), the throstle, (song thrush), the wren and other birds (III.1.118–26).

- Oberon speaks of wilder, more masculine, creatures: lion, pard, bear, wolf, bull, ape and boar (e.g. II.1.180–81).

- The lovers are linked to flowers and nature too (e.g. I.1.185, 215) in the form of roses and virgin thorns, primroses, green wheat and hawthorn buds.

- The flower images are continued comically in the workmen's play with references to 'flowers of odious savours sweet' (III.1.75)a 'cherry nose', 'yellow cowslip cheeks' and eyes 'green as leeks' (V.1.323–7).

It is a play set in three worlds, with three stories running through it, yet these powerful images draw the strands of the play together. Just as the groups of characters temporarily inhabit the world occupied by each of the other groups, so the crossover of the images helps to create a sense of unity between the three worlds.

COMEDY

Though the events of the play sometimes seem dangerous and threatening, and there is considerable dramatic tension at times, the knowledge that there is a power that can resolve things happily in the end enables the comic aspects of the play to dominate. The exaggerated language of the lovers and the workmen's awkward attempts at verse are clear pointers to the comedy, which is the essence of the play.

Now take a break!

PART FOUR

RESOURCES

HOW TO USE QUOTATIONS

One of the secrets of success in writing essays is the way you use quotations. There are five basic principles:

❶ Put inverted commas at the beginning and end of the quotation.

❷ Write the quotation exactly as it appears in the original.

❸ Do not use a quotation that repeats what you have just written.

❹ Use the quotation so that it fits into your sentence.

❺ Keep the quotation as short as possible.

Quotations should be used to develop the line of thought in your essays. Your comment should not duplicate what is in your quotation. For example:

Lysander tells Helena that Demetrius loves Hermia not Helena, 'Demetrius loves her, and he loves not you'. (III.2.136)

Far more effective is to write:

Lysander tells Helena that Demetrius loves Hermia 'and he loves not you'.

Always lay out the lines as they appear in the text. For example:

When Demetrius wakes he falls instantly in love with Helena, declaring:
'O Helen, goddess, nymph, perfect, divine –
To what, my love, shall I compare thine eyne?' (III.2.137–8)

However, the most sophisticated way of using the writer's words is to embed them into your sentence:

Puck describes how he came across a 'crew of patches, rude mechanicals' (III.2.10) rehearsing a play near where Titania was sleeping.

When you use quotations in this way, you are demonstrating the ability to use text as evidence to support your ideas – not simply including words from the original to prove you have read it.

COURSEWORK ESSAY

Set aside an hour or so at the start of your work to plan what you have to do.

- List all the points you feel are needed to cover the task. Collect page references of information and quotations that will support what you have to say. A helpful tool is the highlighter pen: this saves painstaking copying and enables you to target precisely what you want to use.

- Focus on what you consider to be the main points of the essay. Try to sum up your argument in a single sentence, which could be the closing sentence of your essay. Depending on the essay title, it could be a statement about a character: Of all the characters in *A Midsummer Night's Dream*, Helena is the one with whom we can most easily sympathise because, being the most steadfast in her love, she suffers the most and yet still ends up with someone who does not really love her of his own free will; an opinion about setting: Shakespeare set much of the play in a moonlit wood to emphasise the mysterious, frightening and dream-like qualities of the events; or a judgement on a theme: I think that the main theme of *A Midsummer Night's Dream* is love because most of the characters in the play experience this emotion in one form or another.

- Make a short essay plan. Use the first paragraph to introduce the argument you wish to make. In the following paragraphs develop this argument with details, examples and other possible points of view. Sum up your argument in the last paragraph. Check you have answered the question.

- Write the essay, remembering all the time the central point you are making.

- On completion, go back over what you have written to eliminate careless errors and improve expression. Read it aloud to yourself, or, if you are feeling more confident, to a relative or friend.

If you can, try to type your essay, using a word processor. This will allow you to correct and improve your writing without spoiling its appearance.

SITTING THE EXAMINATION

Examination papers are carefully designed to give you the opportunity to do your best. Follow these handy hints for exam success:

BEFORE YOU START

- Make sure you know the subject of the examination so that you are properly prepared and equipped.

- You need to be comfortable and free from distractions. Inform the invigilator if anything is off-putting, e.g. a shaky desk.

- Read the instructions, or rubric, on the front of the examination paper. You should know by now what you have to do but check to reassure yourself.

EXAMINER'S SECRET
Always spend most time on questions that offer most marks.

- Observe the time allocation – and follow it carefully. If they recommend 60 minutes for Question 1 and 30 minutes for Question 2, it is because Question 1 carries twice as many marks.

- Consider the mark allocation. You should write a longer response for 4 marks than for 2 marks.

WRITING YOUR RESPONSES

- Use the questions to structure your response, e.g. question: 'The endings of X's poems are always particularly significant. Explain their importance with reference to two poems.' The first part of your answer will describe the ending of the first poem; the second part will look at the ending of the second poem; the third part will be an explanation of the significance of the two endings.

EXAMINER'S SECRET
Always read the whole examination paper before you start writing.

- Write a brief draft outline of your response.

- A typical 30-minute examination essay is probably between 400 and 600 words in length.

- Keep your writing legible and easy to read, using paragraphs to show the structure of your answers.

- Spend a couple of minutes afterwards quickly checking for obvious errors.

WHEN YOU HAVE FINISHED

- Don't be downhearted – if you found the examination difficult, it is probably because you really worked at the questions. Let's face it, they are not meant to be easy!

- Don't pay too much attention to what your friends have to say about the paper. Everyone's experience is different and no two people ever give the same answers.

IMPROVE YOUR GRADE

Whether you are writing a coursework essay or answering a question in an examination, there are certain things that will help you to achieve the best grade that you can. A good essay will show you understand various aspects of the play. You will need to show that you have a good knowledge of the following:

EXAMINER'S SECRET
Examiners read everything written down even if you have crossed it out – so put a line through notes, never obliterate them.

- PLOT: the story-line of the play, the order in which things happen and the way the events are organised

- CHARACTERS: how they are revealed to us by what they do, what they say and what others say about them, their relationships to each other and how they change in the course of the play

- ATMOSPHERE: how this is created over the course of the play, through the stage directions, changes of setting, the way characters react to each other, and the use of special effects. How do these things affect or reflect what is happening?

- CONTEXT: the influences on the playwright. This may be what has already happened, what is currently happening in their lives, and/or what they hope, or fear, may happen in the future. In their writing they may reflect or contradict the views, opinions and beliefs of other people. Try to consider the writer's views, and comment on the social and historical context in which the writer was working.

A D–GRADE RESPONSE

In awarding your essay a D grade, the examiner will have considered that you:

- Showed understanding of the different layers of meaning in the play

- Made useful points which you supported with textual evidence

- Showed understanding of the social conditions at the time in which the play was set

- Showed understanding of the culture at the time the play was set

You will also have shown that you understand:

- Some of the dramatic effects of what the characters did and said

- The effect created by the structure of the play and the dramatic devices that the playwright used.

The **key word** for a D grade is **understanding**.

IMPROVE YOUR GRADE TO A C

To raise your grade to a C you need to show the examiner that you:

- Have insight into how the playwright puts his different meanings and ideas across through the language and the structure of the play

- Can use appropriate details to support your views

- Can set out your ideas in effective ways

- Can write clearly about how the historical, cultural and social setting affects our understanding of the play.

You will have also shown insight into:

EXAMINER'S SECRET
Always check your answer when you have finished.

CHECK THE BOOK

W.H. Smith have a video 'Shakespeare – The Life of William Shakespeare' (Castle Communications Ltd, 1995) which comes with a book. The video and book pack looks at the society in which Shakespeare lived.

- The dramatic effects of the characters and the action
- The effects of the dramatic devices and the structure of the play

For example, instead of writing,

> **When Egeus brings Hermia before Theseus, the Duke has to make an important decision and he supports Egeus**

you can say:

> **When Egeus arrives at the court 'Full of vexation' because Hermia has refused to marry Demetrius, Theseus is placed in a difficult position. The law, however, is clear; and Theseus must uphold the law so he supports Egeus.**

Be selective with your quotations, and if possible try to make cross-references with other parts of the play.

The key word for a C grade is **insight**.

IMPROVE YOUR GRADE TO AN A/A*

To raise your grade to an A or A* you have to show that you

- Have written clearly argued responses which are
  - original
  - coherent
  - enthusiastic
  - sensitive

- Can analyse and interpret the importance of such things as the social and historical setting of the play

- Can analyse and interpret the cultural and literary tradition from which the writer comes

You will also have shown an original approach when analysing and interpreting:

- The dramatic effects created by the characters, by what they say, by what they do, and by what happens to them

- The way the playwright structures the play, the way events lead on from one another, and where there are particularly dramatic moments or a particular theme is developed

- The playwright's use of dramatic devices, including lighting changes, the sort of stage set, and the use of particular sorts of language

EXAMINER'S SECRET

Plan your answers, then you do not repeat yourself or waffle!

An A-grade candidate would develop the above statement about Theseus's decision, so it looks something like this:

> When Egeus arrives at the court he admits that he is 'Full of vexation' at Hermia's refusal to marry Demetrius. Accusing Lysander of winning Hermia's affections with underhanded tricks, he demands his 'ancient privilege' to dispose of his daughter to the man that he has chosen, which suggests a time when a daughter's rights would have little importance. Egeus is too angry to think clearly and only sees his own side of the situation. This places Theseus in a difficult position. As the ruler he must uphold the law and support Egeus, but being in love himself he might have liked to allow Hermia and Lysander to follow their own hearts. He is careful to give Hermia time to consider her answer, and by pointing out the penalties for refusal he tries to persuade her to agree to her father's wishes. Her refusal to do so leads to her eloping with Lysander to avoid the laws of Athens.

This answer interprets and analyses Shakespeare's intentions. Instead of just making a statement about a character and an event, there is an interpretation of Theseus's motives, analysis of the language Shakespeare uses, and reference to what has gone before and to what may follow. There is not only observation, but a line of thought is also presented which explores the language, the characters and the events of the play against the social and cultural background of the time in which it is set.

The key words for an A/A* grade are **originality**, **analysis** and **interpretation**.

EXAMINER'S SECRET

Examiners never take marks away.

You may be thinking that some (or even all!) of this sounds a bit beyond you. Don't worry – have a go at planning, preparing, developing and checking your answer really carefully. It is possible for anyone to improve their work if they follow this advice. You might be in for a very pleasant surprise!

SAMPLE ESSAY PLAN

A typical essay question on *A Midsummer Night's Dream* is followed by a sample essay plan in note form. This does not represent the only answer to the question, merely one answer. Do not be afraid to include your own ideas, and leave out some of those in the sample! Remember that quotations are essential to prove and illustrate the points you make.

To what extent is Theseus presented as a good ruler?

Such a question anticipates a carefully focused response. To show 'to what extent' you will need to consider:

- What might be regarded as desirable qualities in a ruler

- Whether Theseus demonstrates these qualities

- The historical context of the play

- The role of Theseus within the context of the play

- His behaviour in contrast to the behaviour of others

INTRODUCTION
This should clearly outline how you are going to deal with the question, and could include a brief idea of how you will interpret the key term 'good ruler'. You could list the qualities which would have been considered desirable in Elizabethan times – and perhaps contrast them with the duties of a modern day ruler.

FIRST IMPRESSIONS
How our impressions of Theseus are first created:

- He opens the play, which gives him an immediately dominant position.

- His love for Hippolyta gives him humanity.

THESEUS AS UPHOLDER OF THE LAW

- His support of Egeus shows support of the law.

- He sees the law as of first importance.

- He appears to be harsh.

HIS GENTLER NATURE

- His offer of an alternative penalty to death suggests he is fair-minded.

- He approaches problems calmly – he is judicious.

- His language is measured and thoughtful.

- He offers Hermia time to decide.

- He takes Egeus and Demetrius aside to talk to them about the situation.

- Towards the end of the play he overrules Egeus and lets the four lovers marry for love.

- He is approachable – even Bottom feels he may talk to him directly.

CHECK THE BOOK
Have a look at some of Shakespeare's comedies such as *Twelfth Night*, *As You Like It*, *Much Ado About Nothing* or *The Taming of the Shrew*.

THESEUS AS A WELL-ROUNDED MAN

- He enjoys 'royal' pursuits – we see him hunting.

- His description of the sound of the hounds suggests an interest in music.

- He is amused when he discovers the four lovers asleep together.

- He is a patron of the arts, encouraging his subjects to perform their play.

- He has a sense of humour, making witty remarks during the play.

- He appreciates honest effort and will try not to hurt the feelings of others.

CONCLUSION

Draw together all the material that you have used in the main body of your essay, but do not simply reiterate everything you have written. Show whether Theseus matches up to the qualities you had listed in your introduction. Try to add something extra to give your reader something to think about, e.g. that Shakespeare helps us to appreciate Theseus's qualities as a good ruler by providing us with Oberon as a contrast.

This is by no means an exhaustive or definitive answer to the question. However, looked at in conjunction with the other information in the **Resources** section, it does show you the way in which your mind should be working in order to produce a reasonably thorough essay.

FURTHER QUESTIONS

Make a plan as shown above and attempt these questions.

❶ How might a modern production of *A Midsummer Night's Dream* differ from an Elizabethan one?

❷ Examine the characters of Hermia and Helena. Show in what ways they differ and in what ways they are similar.

❸ What different aspects of love do you see as important in the play?

❹ Does Shakespeare's use of unpleasant and possibly threatening scenes add to or spoil our enjoyment of the comedy in this play?

❺ In what ways is this play about 'dreams'?

❻ How do events support Lysander's claim that 'The course of true love never did run smooth'?

❼ Are there any similarities between the fairies and the humans in this play?

❽ If you were directing a production of this play how would you bring out the humour in Act V?

EXAMINER'S SECRET
You will get marks in an examination if you show you have planned your answer.

eration a sequence of repeated consonant
nds

ithesis opposing or contrasting ideas

nk verse unrhymed iambic pentameter, the
st common Shakespearean poetic form

racternym a name that represents its bearer in
ıe appropriate way

nedy a broad description for a drama which is
nded primarily to entertain the audience and
ich ends happily for the characters

ce a form of humorous drama which uses
ggerated characters, absurd and ridiculous
ations and knockabout action to get laughs

ıre the term for a kind or type of literature, e.g.
ıantic novel, short story, play

ıb the commonest metrical foot in English
se, a weak stress followed by a strong stress:
ım

ıbic pentameter a line of five iambic feet. The
st common metrical pattern found in English
se

ıgery word pictures which help our
ıerstanding and interpretation

ıy saying one thing while meaning another. In
ımatic irony the characters are blind to fateful
ːumstances of which the audience is fully
ıre, so that what the characters say has an extra
ıning for the audience

ical using the language of lyric poetry, a form
t expresses a speaker's thoughts and feelings in
ːrsonal and colourful way

metaphor a metaphor is the fusing of two
different things or ideas; one thing is described as
being another thing, e.g. 'O, how ripe in show /
Thy lips – those kissing cherries – tempting grow!'
(III.2.139–40)

metre the pattern of stressed and unstressed
syllables in a line of verse

oxymoron a figure of speech in which words of
opposite meaning are put together

poetic verse a style of speech in Shakespeare's
plays using rhyming couplets and having a strong
rhythm

prologue an introduction to a literary work, or,
in the case of a play the speaker of such an
introduction

prose all writing that is not in verse

pun a play on words

rhyming couplet a pair of lines that rhyme

simile a figure of speech in which one thing is said
to be like another, always containing the word
'like' or 'as'

soliloquy a speech in which a character in a play
speaks directly to the audience – as if thinking
aloud about motives, feelings and decisions

sub-plot a subsidiary action running parallel with
the main plot of a play or novel

9 Oberon describes Puck as a 'mad spirit'. In what ways does his reputation and behaviour support that description?

10 Show how Shakespeare's use of verse and prose helps us to a better understanding of the events and the characters.

CHE(
THE

There is a B
of *A Midsur*
Night's Drea
starring Hel
Mirren, Pete
McEnery an
Davenport.
1988 produc
was produce
Jonathan M
directed by
Moshinsky.

EXA
SEC

You can get
marks in an
examinatio
just two sid
writing – n
write a boc

Now take a break!

CHECKPOINT 1 Young male actors played the parts of women; there was very little scenery; and no special effects.

CHECKPOINT 2 Although Athenian law would condemn Hermia to death, Theseus is lenient. Hermia would be forbidden from marrying anyone else and would have to spend the rest of her life in a convent.

CHECKPOINT 3 There are three conflicts, between: Egeus and Hermia; Egeus and Lysander; Lysander and Demetrius.

CHECKPOINT 4 Bottom interrupts at line 47, because he wants to play Thisbe; and at line 66, when he asks to play the lion too.

CHECKPOINT 5 Act II, Scene 1 – Act III, Scene 2 takes place at night-time, and there are frequent references to night-time throughout these scenes – see how many you can find. However, night is regularly mentioned elsewhere too: consider why this might be.

CHECKPOINT 6 Lysander says that he and Hermia share 'one heart' because he wants to share 'one bed' with her (41–52). The image of two lovers sharing one heart is a traditional one. Lysander then claims to see Helena's heart (105), a metaphor for her emotions. When Hermia says 'Methought a serpent eat my heart away' (149), she presents a violent image of stolen love.

CHECKPOINT 7 Bottom says 'defect' when he means 'effect' (35); he says 'odious' when he means 'odours' (75–6); Flute says 'Ninny's tomb' when he should have said 'Ninus' tomb' (90–91) – 'ninny' means 'idiot'!

CHECKPOINT 8 The workmen hope to perform their play at the wedding celebrations for Theseus and Hippolyta.

CHECKPOINT 9 Demetrius loves Helena (before the start of the play), then Hermia, then Helena again; Lysander loves Hermia, then Helena, and then Hermia again. The women's affections remain constant: Helena loves Demetrius; Hermia loves Lysander.

CHECKPOINT 10 Oberon will 'undo' the spell on Titania (61) and tells Puck to 'take off' the spell on Bottom (79); see also 86–91. Theseus speaks of 'gentle concord' (142); see also 'fortunately' (176), 'Melted' (165). The repetition of the word 'now' (46, 61, 78, 83, 86, 165, 174) indicates that things have changed.

CHECKPOINT 11 The hunting party wakes the four lovers. Demetrius and Helena are in love with one another; so are Lysander and Hermia.

CHECKPOINT 12 Bottom is no longer regarded as a bumbling nuisance; the workmen miss him and praise his talents.

CHECKPOINT 13 The madman sees numerous devils; the lover can see beauty in the face of a gypsy; the poet sees all kinds of imaginary things (7–17).

CHECKPOINT 14 The comedy reminds us of the farcical happenings that have taken place in the woods of *A Midsummer Night's Dream*. Mistakes are made both in the main story and in the workmen's play. The tragic ending of 'Pyramus and Thisby' shows us that events could easily have turned out tragically for the four lovers.

CHECKPOINT 15 The description is sinister: Puck mentions wild animals, screeching owls, graves, and Hecate, the three-headed goddess who commanded evil spirits (see **Classical mythology** in **Themes**). However, it is Puck who is speaking and the tone is light-hearted.

CHECKPOINT 16 Puck uses magic to cause Lysander to love Helena (later the spell is taken off and he loves Hermia again); and magic is used to make Demetrius fall in love with Helena. Oberon uses magic to make Titania (temporarily) fall in love with the first thing she sees when she wakes up (Bottom).

CHECKPOINT 17

- There are musical serenades (I.1.30; 189).

- The fairies sing a lullaby (II.2.1–30).

- Titania asks Bottom if he would like to hear some music (IV.1.27–9).

- Titania dances with Oberon (IV.1.80–85).

- There is imagery in the hunting scene (IV.1.106–27).

- Music is a feature of the wedding celebrations in Act V, Scene 1.

Throughout, music creates a joyful and/or frivolous mood.

CHECKPOINT 18 The moon is mentioned regularly – often it reminds the audience of the night-time setting. The moon may also be a mark of time (I.1.2–6); denote a romantic setting (I.1.30, I.1.209–10, III.1.44–5); or create a particular atmosphere (II.1.103–5, 155–62).

CHECKPOINT 19 Lysander, then Demetrius, is under an illusion that he loves Helena; Titania's love for Bottom is an illusion. The lovers' reactions to the night's happenings are described at IV.1.186–99, and Bottom's reactions at IV.1.199–213: the words 'vision', 'dream', 'wonders' and 'images'/'imagination' are recurrent here, and at V.1.1–127.

CHECKPOINT 20 The tragic aspect of 'Pyramus and Thisbe' is reminiscent of *Romeo and Juliet*.

TEST ANSWERS

TEST YOURSELF (ACT I)

1 Egeus (*Scene 1*)

2 Hermia (*Scene 1*)

3 Helena (*Scene 1*)

4 Helena (*Scene 1*)

5 Flute (*Scene 2*)

6 Philostrate (*Scene 1*)

7 Hermia (*Scene 1*)

8 Theseus (*Scene 1*)

9 Flute (*Scene 2*)

10 Snug (*Scene 2*)

TEST YOURSELF (ACT II)

1 Titania (*Scene 1*)

2 Oberon (*Scene 1*)

3 Puck (*Scene 1*)

4 Helena (*Scene 2*)

5 Hermia (*Scene 2*)

6 Titania (*Scene 1*)

7 Puck (*Scene 1*)

8 Demetrius (*Scene 1*)

9 Helena (*Scene 1*)

10 Helena (*Scene 2*)

TEST YOURSELF (ACT III)

1 Bottom (*Scene 1*)

2 Puck (*Scene 1*)

3 Quince (*Scene 1*)

4 Puck (*Scene 2*)

5 Helena (*Scene 2*)

6 Bottom (*Scene 1*)

7 Hermia (*Scene 2*)

8 Puck (*Scene 2*)

9 Demetrius (*Scene 2*)

10 Helena (*Scene 2*)

TEST YOURSELF (ACT IV)

1 Bottom (*Scene 1*)

2 Oberon (*Scene 1*)

3 Egeus (*Scene 1*)

4 Demetrius (*Scene 1*)

5 Flute (*Scene 2*)

6 Bottom (*Scene 1*)

7 Titania (*Scene 1*)

8 Bottom (*Scene 1*)

9 Oberon (*Scene 1*)

10 Hermia, Lysander, Helena and Demetrius (*Scene 1*)

TEST YOURSELF (ACT V)

1 Theseus

2 Philostrate

3 Hippolyta

4 Theseus

5 Bottom as Pyramus

6 Oberon

7 Hermia, Lysander, Helena and Demetrius

8 Philostrate

9 Hippolyta

10 Bottom as Pyramus

11 Quince as the Prologue

Maya Angelou
I Know Why the Caged Bird Sings

Jane Austen
Pride and Prejudice

Alan Ayckbourn
Absent Friends

Elizabeth Barrett Browning
Selected Poems

Robert Bolt
A Man for All Seasons

Harold Brighouse
Hobson's Choice

Charlotte Brontë
Jane Eyre

Emily Brontë
Wuthering Heights

Shelagh Delaney
A Taste of Honey

Charles Dickens
David Copperfield
Great Expectations
Hard Times
Oliver Twist

Roddy Doyle
Paddy Clarke Ha Ha Ha

George Eliot
Silas Marner
The Mill on the Floss

Anne Frank
The Diary of a Young Girl

William Golding
Lord of the Flies

Oliver Goldsmith
She Stoops to Conquer

Willis Hall
The Long and the Short and the Tall

Thomas Hardy
Far from the Madding Crowd

The Mayor of Casterbridge
Tess of the d'Urbervilles
The Withered Arm and other Wessex Tales

L.P. Hartley
The Go-Between

Seamus Heaney
Selected Poems

Susan Hill
I'm the King of the Castle

Barry Hines
A Kestrel for a Knave

Louise Lawrence
Children of the Dust

Harper Lee
To Kill a Mockingbird

Laurie Lee
Cider with Rosie

Arthur Miller
The Crucible
A View from the Bridge

Robert O'Brien
Z for Zachariah

Frank O'Connor
My Oedipus Complex and Other Stories

George Orwell
Animal Farm

J.B. Priestley
An Inspector Calls
When We Are Married

Willy Russell
Educating Rita
Our Day Out

J.D. Salinger
The Catcher in the Rye

William Shakespeare
Henry IV Part I
Henry V
Julius Caesar

Macbeth
The Merchant of Venice
A Midsummer Night's Dream
Much Ado About Nothing
Romeo and Juliet
The Tempest
Twelfth Night

George Bernard Shaw
Pygmalion

Mary Shelley
Frankenstein

R.C. Sherriff
Journey's End

Rukshana Smith
Salt on the snow

John Steinbeck
Of Mice and Men

Robert Louis Stevenson
Dr Jekyll and Mr Hyde

Jonathan Swift
Gulliver's Travels

Robert Swindells
Daz 4 Zoe

Mildred D. Taylor
Roll of Thunder, Hear My Cry

Mark Twain
Huckleberry Finn

James Watson
Talking in Whispers

Edith Wharton
Ethan Frome

William Wordsworth
Selected Poems

A Choice of Poets

Mystery Stories of the Nineteenth Century including The Signalman

Nineteenth Century Short Stories

Poetry of the First World War

Six Women Poets

MANCAT
COLLEGE LIBRARIES
ASHTON OLD ROAD
MANCHESTER
M11 2WH

MANCAT
Wythenshawe Sixth Form
Newall Green Centre
Greenbow Road
Wythenshawe
MANCHESTER
M23 2SX

Margaret Atwood
Cat's Eye
The Handmaid's Tale

Jane Austen
Emma
Mansfield Park
Persuasion
Pride and Prejudice
Sense and Sensibility

Alan Bennett
Talking Heads

William Blake
Songs of Innocence and of Experience

Charlotte Brontë
Jane Eyre
Villette

Emily Brontë
Wuthering Heights

Angela Carter
Nights at the Circus

Geoffrey Chaucer
The Franklin's Prologue and Tale
The Miller's Prologue and Tale
The Prologue to the Canterbury Tales
The Wife of Bath's Prologue and Tale

Samuel Coleridge
Selected Poems

Joseph Conrad
Heart of Darkness

Daniel Defoe
Moll Flanders

Charles Dickens
Bleak House
Great Expectations
Hard Times

Emily Dickinson
Selected Poems

John Donne
Selected Poems

Carol Ann Duffy
Selected Poems

George Eliot
Middlemarch
The Mill on the Floss

T.S. Eliot
Selected Poems
The Waste Land

F. Scott Fitzgerald
The Great Gatsby

E.M. Forster
A Passage to India

Brian Friel
Translations

Thomas Hardy
Jude the Obscure
The Mayor of Casterbridge
The Return of the Native
Selected Poems
Tess of the d'Urbervilles

Seamus Heaney
Selected Poems from 'Opened Ground'

Nathaniel Hawthorne
The Scarlet Letter

Homer
The Iliad
The Odyssey

Aldous Huxley
Brave New World

Kazuo Ishiguro
The Remains of the Day

Ben Jonson
The Alchemist

James Joyce
Dubliners

John Keats
Selected Poems

Christopher Marlowe
Doctor Faustus
Edward II

Arthur Miller
Death of a Salesman

John Milton
Paradise Lost Books I & II

Toni Morrison
Beloved

George Orwell
Nineteen Eighty-Four

Sylvia Plath
Selected Poems

Alexander Pope
Rape of the Lock & Selected Poems

William Shakespeare
Antony and Cleopatra
As You Like It
Hamlet
Henry IV Part I
King Lear
Macbeth
Measure for Measure
The Merchant of Venice
A Midsummer Night's Dream
Much Ado About Nothing
Othello
Richard II
Richard III
Romeo and Juliet
The Taming of the Shrew
The Tempest
Twelfth Night
The Winter's Tale

George Bernard Shaw
Saint Joan

Mary Shelley
Frankenstein

Jonathan Swift
Gulliver's Travels and A Modest Proposal

Alfred Tennyson
Selected Poems

Virgil
The Aeneid

Alice Walker
The Color Purple

Oscar Wilde
The Importance of Being Earnest

Tennessee Williams
A Streetcar Named Desire

Jeanette Winterson
Oranges Are Not the Only Fruit

John Webster
The Duchess of Malfi

Virginia Woolf
To the Lighthouse

W.B. Yeats
Selected Poems

Metaphysical Poets≥

THE ULTIMATE WEB SITE FOR THE ULTIMATE LITERATURE GUIDES

At York Notes we believe in helping you achieve exam success. Log on to **www.yorknotes.com** and see how we have made revision even easier, with over 300 titles available to download twenty-four hours a day. The downloads have lots of additional features such as pop-up boxes providing instant glossary definitions, user-friendly links to every part of the guide, and scanned illustrations offering visual appeal. All you need to do is log on to **www.yorknotes.com** and download the books you need to help you achieve exam success.

KEY FEATURES:

Details on how York Notes can help you

Menu Bar to help you find your way around the site

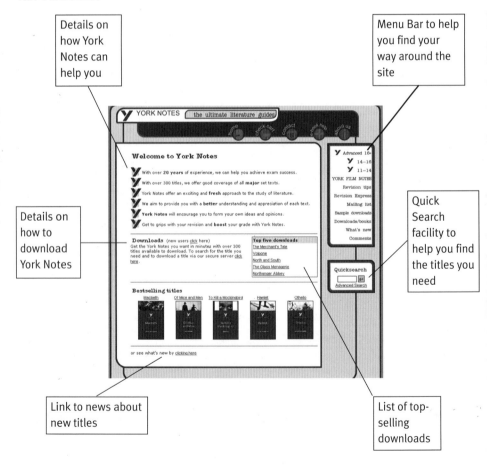

Details on how to download York Notes

Quick Search facility to help you find the titles you need

Link to news about new titles

List of top-selling downloads